Change the Shame

Continuing the Battle for Civil Rights

Small Group Study Edition

By
Perry Underwood

Edited by Rob Fischer

Change the Shame
Small Group Study Edition

ISBN-13: 978-1499325904
ISBN-10: 1499325908

Published by
Fischer Publishing

Acknowledgements

I'd like to express my sincere appreciation to Rob Fischer, Kass McHugh, Kim Gardell and the team at Bassett & Brush for their invaluable assistance in making this book possible.

I'd also like to thank Annette, Erika and Courtney for helping me see things more clearly.

Table of Contents

Introduction

"Those who don't know history are destined to repeat it."

—Edmund Burke (1729-1797)

The second paragraph of the ***Declaration of Independence*** begins with the following statement:

> *We hold these truths to be self-evident, that all Men are created equal, that they are endowed by their Creator with certain unalienable Rights, that among these are Life, Liberty, and the Pursuit of Happiness...*

Consider the power of this statement for a moment. The founders of the United States of America believed that all Men were born with God-given Rights to be alive, free and pursue the things that provided happiness.

Ironically, when this Declaration was written, slavery was prevalent in this nation and freedoms of women were extremely limited compared with the freedoms of men. But history has repeatedly confirmed that the authors of this **Declaration of Independence** were "spot on" at the time the document was written.

Those who penned this great document described the Rights of Freedom and Liberty they believed to be theirs. Probably without realizing it, they were laying the foundation for these same Rights to be extended to and enjoyed by all. This foundational truth— that we all have God-given Rights to be alive, free and pursue happiness— has been the guiding light of this great nation for almost 250 years.

On December 6, 1865, almost ninety years after the **Declaration of Independence**, the Thirteenth Amendment to the **U.S. Constitution** was ratified. Section 1 of this Amendment states:

> *Neither slavery nor involuntary servitude, except as a punishment for crime whereof the party shall have been duly convicted, shall exist within the United States, or any place subject to their jurisdiction.*

This Amendment was the beginning of a long and tumultuous process of changing the way the people of this nation viewed freedom and liberty.

After writing the **Declaration of Independence,** it took our nation almost ninety years to recognize that the Right of Liberty expressed by our Founding Fathers was a Right of *all* men, not just the wealthy or the white. If what was written in 1776 was true at that time, then it had to be true throughout all time.

But we are slow learners. Many white men were still oppressing and making life difficult for former slaves and anyone with dark skin. Even though slaves and all men were now free, additional Amendments to the **U.S. Constitution** were needed to provide the opportunity for these former slaves to enjoy their new-found freedom and pursue happiness.

On July 9, 1868, the Fourteenth Amendment was ratified. This Amendment gave *citizenship* to all persons born or naturalized in the United States.

On February 3, 1870, the Fifteenth Amendment to the **U.S. Constitution** was ratified. This Amendment gave all citizens (men) the right to vote.

But what about women? Just because a woman was in a body different from man's, is that any reason to limit her freedoms, rights and privileges? By now it was well established that the difference in the color of one's skin was no reason to deny men their God-given Rights. Could it be true that women, too, should be entitled to these same Rights?

Even after all our nation had been through to end slavery and grant voting Rights to black men, some still held to ideals that suppressed members of our society, denying Rights to those of a different gender.

The ***Declaration of Independence*** also states:

> *That to secure these Rights, Governments are instituted among Men, deriving their just Powers from the Consent of the Governed....*

Therefore, if women are to be governed, along with men, then consent of the government must come from women as well. On August 20, 1920, fifty years after black men were given the Right to vote, women and all citizens of appropriate age were granted this precious Right.

We're starting to see a pattern here. The unalienable Rights outlined in the ***Declaration of Independence*** keep coming back to correct us. Slavery, denying the Right of black men to vote, and denying the Right of women to vote: each of these were a matter of *injustice*. Injustice, because no matter how strongly one tried to defend his or her point of view, at the end of the day, fellow human beings were deprived of their God-given Rights of Life, Liberty, and the Pursuit of Happiness.

But what happens when one person's rights conflict with another person's Rights? As a restaurant owner, one has the right to do business with whomever they choose. Should one be forced to serve food to someone they don't like? As a property owner, one has the right to lease or rent to whomever they wish. Should one be forced to rent property to someone who doesn't fit in with the color of the neighborhood?

As a smoker, one has the right to smoke wherever he or she pleases. Should one be deprived of his or her happiness just because some killjoy doesn't like the smell of smoke? The Right of freedom of speech gives me the right to say whatever I want, whenever I please. Why should I be denied the right to say whatever I want about another individual or shout "Fire!" in a crowded theater as a practical joke?

Once again, we find the answers to these questions in the enduring wisdom of the ***Declaration of Independence***. Certain Rights are said to be "unalienable," which means they cannot be lost or taken away. In other words, no matter what one's rights may be, certain Rights cannot be "lost" or "trumped" by the rights of another.

You may have already noticed but the word right or rights sometimes have an upper case "R" and other times a lower case "r". We all possess rights but those Rights spoken of in the ***Declaration of Independence*** and granted in the ***U.S. Constitution*** are identified by the upper case "R" as they are Unalienable Rights that cannot be trumped.

Time and again, the justice system of our nation has established that certain rights of individuals are inferior to the "Unalienable Rights" of another. These

"Unalienable Rights" have come to be known as "Civil Liberties," "Civil Rights," or "Human Rights."

The right of a man to own slaves is trumped by the slaves' Right of Liberty. The right of a Restaurateur to serve only whites is trumped by the Civil Rights of equality for the black man. The right of the property owner to refuse to rent to families with children is trumped by the Civil Rights of the family seeking to rent a home.

For Black Americans and other minorities, it took almost two hundred years after the writing of the ***Declaration of Independence*** and one hundred years after the **U.S. Constitution** granted their freedom for their Civil Rights to be codified into law. In 1964, a Civil Rights Law was passed making it illegal to discriminate based on race, color, religion, sex, or national origin. Familial status, age and disability were other protected classes added to this list through the passage of other Civil Rights laws throughout the years.

Throughout our history we seem to eventually figure it out. Every person has the Right to Life, Liberty, and the Pursuit of Happiness and no rights of another can ever trump these Rights. But getting it correct has been difficult and has come at great cost. It took a Civil War, a Suffrage Movement, and a Civil Rights Movement to awaken our leadership and the people of our nation to the injustice of the day.

Why must we insist on punishing ourselves with such injustice for generations, only to be finally cured at such horrific cost? But we're doing it to ourselves again.

Today, as a nation, we are facing another great injustice. For fifty years, tens of millions have suffered severely under this injustice. For fifty years, the rights of one individual have trampled the Unalienable Rights of another. For fifty years, those who have spoken out against this injustice have themselves been marginalized and ignored.

There will be no more begging or pleading. The opportunity for a quiet end to the injustice is now gone; it is time for war. We are about to embark on a Second Civil War. This Second Civil War will **NOT** be fought on battlefields or with guns and canons. Those fighting against this injustice must do so **WITHOUT** violence, the taking of lives, or the destruction of property. This Second Civil War will be fought in the marketplace, in the polls, and in the hearts and minds of the American people. The first Civil War needed bullets and bayonets; the Second Civil war will be fought with dollars and votes.

It took four years of battle for justice to triumph in the first Civil War and it took another one hundred years for those freed to have equality. This Second Civil War may require a lengthier battle, but equality and justice will be instantaneous once this war has been won. Let us not rest until we are victorious!

GROUP DISCUSSION— *Introduction*

Do you REALLY believe that in the eyes of God, all men are created equal?

If not, why?

Have you ever experienced a situation where you felt your Civil Rights were violated or that you were discriminated against because of race, religion, sex, age or disability?

If so, briefly describe that situation.

How did you feel at the time?

Have you ever discriminated against another person in a way that may have violated their Civil Rights?

If so, briefly describe that situation.

How do you feel about that today and in what way would you behave differently?

CHAPTER ONE

The Great Divide

"I believe that to have interfered as I have done, as I have always freely admitted, I have done in behalf of His despised poor, was not wrong, but right. Now, if it is deemed necessary that I should forfeit my life for the furtherance of the ends of justice, and mingle my blood further with the blood of my children and with the blood of millions in this slave country whose rights are disregarded by wicked, cruel, and unjust enactments, I submit; so let it be done!"

—John Brown 1859

Today, it is hard to imagine that the educated citizens of a modern, civilized nation could possibly ignore, condone, or worse yet, participate in the ownership of human beings. Slavery essentially strips other humans of personhood, declaring them non-persons. But slavery was the accepted culture of the United State just a few generations ago.

The *Declaration of Independence* states that all Men are created equal and have the Rights to Life, Liberty, and the Pursuit of Happiness. But during the period when this great document was written, liberty was not a reality for everyone in this nation.

Slavery wasn't outlawed in the State of New York until 1799, or in New Jersey until 1804. But as more and more Americans began to recognize slavery as an injustice, it became clear that the United States was becoming more and more divided over this issue.

In 1812 there were nine "Slave" States and nine "Free" States. Great pains were taken to maintain the balance between these opposing convictions. The *Missouri Compromise of 1820* and the *Compromise of 1850* attempted to bridge this divide by predetermining which lands would be added as free and which would permit slavery. States were added in pairs — one free and one slave — so that no side could gain political advantage over the other.

As time moved on, the rift between the "Slave" and "Free" States became increasingly broad. On the one side, there were those who promoted slavery and were willing to defend it as their right and their way of life. On the other side, there were those who saw slavery for the injustice that it was, but felt powerless to do anything about it.

Year after year this great divide continued to grow as the political machine kept kicking the proverbial can down the road, leaving the problem for future generations to deal with.

Just prior to 1850, there were fifteen "Free" States and fifteen "Slave" States. So when California was added in 1850 as a "Free" State, balance between the conflicting sides was threatened. In the end, the balance was maintained when California appointed a "Pro-slavery" Senator.

Fifty years of bridging the divide and maintaining this delicate balance began to unravel when Congress passed the ***Kansas-Nebraska Act of 1854***. This Act created the territories of Kansas and Nebraska and opened the lands to settlement by pioneers. The Act also established that the question of slavery would be determined through "Popular Sovereignty" which allowed the settlers of these territories to make the choice to be "Free" or "Slave" States. Interestingly enough, slaves were not given a choice or permitted to cast their vote.

Just how divided this nation was over slavery became abundantly clear as Kansas turned into a battleground. Pro-slavery and Pro-freedom proponents alike tried to gain control and impose their will on the other. Kansas came to be called "Bleeding Kansas" for the bloodshed taking place through violent confrontations over slavery.

Upon hearing of the threats to his Pro-freedom family by Pro-slavery ruffians, John Brown, an abolitionist from the State of New York, decided to take matters into his own hands.

Brown quickly gained fame and popularity among slavery abolitionists for his involvement in attacks against, and skirmishes with, Pro-slavery groups in Kansas. Later, Brown traveled back to New York and revealed a plan he had devised to free the slaves. His plan was to start in Virginia and spread throughout the rest of the South by arming slaves and leading a rebellion.

On October 16, 1859, Brown and a group of twenty abolitionists raided and easily took control of the Federal Armory in Harpers Ferry, where 100,000 muskets and rifles were stored. However, the rebellion Brown had planned to free the slaves never got off the ground, as local Pro-slavery farmers quickly organized and prevented Brown and his raiders from being able to leave the Armory.

Several of Brown's men were killed in the gun battle that followed, and a handful escaped. Brown and the remaining abolitionists were arrested and moved to a nearby town in Virginia to await trial. Brown and his surviving raiders were quickly convicted and sentenced to be hanged.

While waiting to be hanged, John Brown was interviewed by newspaper reporters from all over the nation. To some, John Brown was a villain; to others, he was a heroic martyr. To those who had ignored or denied it, the presence and magnitude of this great divide over slavery was now irrefutable. Nothing short of a Civil War would bring the two sides together.

One year after the hanging of John Brown, the first of eleven "Slave" States declared secession from the United States. A few months later the United States was torn by Civil War.

No matter your opinion of John Brown, one thing is undeniable: the people of the United States were greatly divided over slavery and John Brown brought awareness of that division. Slavery was now in the forefront of the minds of all American people.

People could no longer be ignorant or apathetic. When it came to slavery, one had to know where one stood and why, because a day would not go by without slavery being discussed in routine conversations. This nation was greatly divided, and like a powder keg, ready to explode. John Brown was the spark that caused the explosion.

If John Brown had not taken a stand and been that spark, someone else would have been. Those who recognized the injustice in dehumanizing others could no longer sit still. Abolitionist ranks had been growing by the thousands while those in the "Slave" States resolved to dig their heels in deeper. A great many abolitionists were so frustrated over their inability to end the injustice of slavery that something *had* to happen. How tragic that the abolition of slavery came at such great cost; 750,000 Americans died in the Civil War over the injustice of slavery.

So, why the brief history lesson? History has much to teach us, but if we don't pay attention to these lessons we are doomed to repeat them. History has taught us that when a nation is guilty of a great injustice, any compromises and negotiations that *permit* the injustice to continue only serve to *delay the inevitable* and *increase the chances* of prolonged violence and destruction.

History has taught us that injustice will thrive as long as good people remain apathetic and unwilling to pay the price necessary to remedy the injustice. History has taught us that good people must come to the defense of the victims of injustice when those victims have no voice or means for defending themselves.

History has taught us that as previous generations have paid the price for our freedoms, now we bear responsibility to pay the price of freedoms for future generations. History has taught us that those who stand for justice will be ridiculed, mocked, and scoffed at by those benefiting from the injustice. Injustice breeds injustice. History has taught us that those profiting from injustice will not change until tremendous pain has been inflicted upon them.

But most importantly, history has taught us that at the end of the battle, justice will prevail.

GROUP DISCUSSION— *The Great Divide*

If you were an adult living in the U.S. during the 1850s, do you think you would be Pro-Slavery or Anti-Slavery?

Why?

Do you think that John Brown was justified in his attempt to end slavery? Was he a hero or a villain?

Why?

What do you think about the Author's claim that previous generations have paid the price for our Freedoms and we have the responsibility to pay the price for the Freedoms of future generations?

Can you think of a situation where you defended the Rights of another?

If so, describe it:

If you were to encounter injustice in the future, describe your willingness to defend the Rights of others:

Read Acts 15:1-21. Conflict is nothing new. The early church was in conflict over the issue of circumcision; how did they resolve the conflict? ....

....

....

....

....

When the laws of a government are in conflict with the laws of God or the teachings of Christ, how are Christians to respond? ....

....

....

....

....

CHAPTER TWO
I Have A Dream

"The ultimate measure of a man is not where he stands in moments of comfort and convenience, but where he stands at times of challenge and controversy."

—Martin Luther King, Jr.

In 1857 the U.S. Supreme Court made a decision that has come to be known as the **Dred Scott Decision.** This decision held that the federal government had no power to regulate slavery in the territories, and that people of African descent (both slave and free) were not U.S. citizens and therefore not protected by the **U.S. Constitution**. This decision is widely regarded as the worst decision ever made by the U.S. Supreme Court; as we will learn later, it was not.

In 1865, after great sacrifice by thousands of abolitionists, four years of Civil War, and the loss of 750,000 lives, slavery was ended with the ratification of the

Thirteenth Amendment to the U.S. Constitution. In 1868, three years later, the Fourteenth Amendment granted US citizenship to all persons born or naturalized in the USA, and in 1870 the Fifteenth Amendment gave all male citizens the Right to vote.

Even with these great advances for Black Americans over this five year period, there was still a very long way to go. In 1892, a man named Homer Plessy--who was 7/8 Caucasian descent and 1/8 African descent--bought a first-class train ticket from New Orleans to Covington, Louisiana. Upon learning that Plessy was 1/8 African, he was ordered to give up his seat and move to the train car for the "colored" passengers. Plessy refused and was arrested. He appealed his case all the way to the US Supreme Court, where he lost. In the case of **Plessy vs. Ferguson** in 1896, the U.S. Supreme Court upheld the constitutionality of state laws requiring racial segregation. From this case came the doctrine of "Separate but Equal".

In another blunder of equal magnitude, the U.S. Supreme Court affirmed a lower court's decision that Richmond County could use taxpayer dollars to fund a "White Only" high school system. This occurred in the 1899 case of **Cumming vs. Richmond County Board of Education**. This decision expanded the "Separate but Equal" doctrine into the educational system.

With Supreme Court decisions backing up the "Separate but Equal" doctrine, laws requiring segregation of Blacks were untouchable not only in education and transportation, but in every aspect of life. Segregation was common in housing, hotels, restaurants, public restrooms, workplaces, and even churches. Segregation was a way of life throughout the United States, but even more pronounced in the Southern States. For the next fifty-five years, the Civil Liberties of black and other minorities were trampled upon by others with the full blessing and backing of the U.S. Supreme Court.

While discrimination against Black Americans was commonplace, battles for Americans deprived of Civil Rights were still being won. U.S. women won a major Civil Rights victory in 1920 when they were granted the right to vote with the ratification of the Nineteenth Amendment to the **U.S. Constitution**. The Fifteenth Amendment gave voting rights to the black man in 1870, but it was another eighty-five years before Black Americans scored another national victory in Equal Rights and Liberties.

In 1954, the US Supreme Court handed down a decision in the case of **Brown v. Board of Education,** in which the plaintiffs charged that the education of black children in separate public schools from their white counterparts was unconstitutional, and set in motion the future overturning of the "Separate but Equal" doctrine. Many consider this decision to be the beginning of the "African-American Civil Rights Movement."

Although rehearsing these details of U.S. History may seem tedious, these events are extremely important. These events establish how amazingly difficult it has been for some groups or demographic to have their basic Civil Rights recognized by political leaders, and even by the U.S. Supreme Court.

This nation was founded on the premise that individuals possess "Unalienable Rights," and our representative government is responsible to protect those rights. But recognizing the Civil Rights inherent in our Constitution and codifying those Civil Rights into law has been painfully slow and arduous!

We are fools to think that this process will be any less difficult today. Freedom and Civil Rights have only come at great cost by, and through those who were *relentless* in their pursuit of liberty and justice for all.

Rosa Parks and Martin Luther King Jr. are two well-known examples of the price paid for Civil Rights, and how injustice was overcome by the tenacity of a committed few.

For most Americans today it is inconceivable that a city bus system would have separate seating for white and black passengers, and even less conceivable that black passengers would be required to give up their seat to white passengers in the event that the white seating was full. In 1955 this was the law in Montgomery, Alabama. On December 1, 1955, defying the order of the bus driver, a forty-two year old black woman named Rosa Parks refused to give up her seat. Parks was arrested, tried, convicted of disorderly conduct and lost her job as a seamstress at a local department store.

Rosa Parks was not the first Black American to refuse to relinquish their seat and be arrested for their defiance but this time Montgomery, Alabama had picked a fight with the wrong individual.

At the time of her arrest in 1955 Rosa Parks was the secretary of the Montgomery Chapter of the National Association for the Advancement of Colored People (NAACP). As secretary for this organization, Parks was well connected to many of the black leaders of Montgomery.

In response to Parks' arrest, fifty Black American leaders from the Montgomery area, led by Martin Luther King Jr., organized the Montgomery Bus Boycott. It is estimated that ninety percent of Montgomery blacks participated in this boycott creating an eighty percent reduction in bus revenues. After 381 days, the boycott ended in 1956, after a federal court ordered the desegregation of the Montgomery bus system.

As leader of the Montgomery Bus Boycott, the young eloquent minister, Martin Luther King Jr., gained national attention. What had started a year earlier, "The African-American Civil Rights Movement" had found itself a leader in King. On August 23, 1963, King delivered one of the greatest modern-day speeches in what has become known as the "I Have a Dream" speech.

If you have never heard this speech in its entirety you may do so at: *http://www.youtube.com/watch?v=1UV1fs8lAbg* or use this QR code to view it on your mobile device.

Get the free mobile app at
http://gettag.mobi

Thanks to the efforts of King and thousands of others, today black and other minorities enjoy the same Civil Liberties as all other nationalities that make up this blended nation. Although fifty years have passed since Dr. King gave this speech, we still feel the shame of the injustice that prompted it. And yet every accusation of injustice levied by King in this incredible speech is still experienced by another group of American citizens today.

It took an African-American Civil Rights Movement to secure legal recognition of the Civil Rights of Black Americans. It took a Suffrage Movement to grant women the right to vote. These "Movements" were successful because those being unjustly treated had *voices* and were able to rise up in unity and say, "Enough is enough."

These "Movements" were successful because those being unjustly treated had *faces* and those treating them unjustly had to look them in the eyes when they claimed, "You are not equal to me." These "Movements" were successful because those being unjustly treated had *economic power* and with that the ability to inflict financial pain on those treating them unjustly. These "Movements" were successful because those being unjustly treated had the ability to *organize and unite*, making the magnitude of their voices even louder. They were able to turn their individual faces into a sea of faces that could no longer be ignored.

In contrast, the American citizens being unjustly treated today *have no voice* to scream, "Enough is enough." The American citizens being unjustly treated today *have no faces* or eyes to gaze into as we claim, "You are not equal to me". The American citizens being unjustly treated today have *no economic power* and no means to inflict financial pain on those treating them unjustly. The American citizens being unjustly treated today have *no ability to organize or unite* so that they might be heard and seen.

The injustice of our day can only be overcome by a Second Civil War in which abolitionists by the millions rise up and declare on behalf of those who have no voice, "Enough is enough!"

What has been the **SHAME** of the past two generations must be **CHANGED**. No longer will a group of Americans be denied their Unalienable Rights to "Life, Liberty and the Pursuit of Happiness." We must no longer allow the so-called "rights" of some to continue to trample on the Civil Rights of others. We must be their voice. We must be their faces. We must inflict financial pain on their behalf. And we must organize and unite so that together we are heard and seen by those who support or ignore this injustice.

We have a dream: a dream where "Liberty and Justice for all" truly represents the core value of the Country we pledge our allegiance to. A dream where we honor the words of our founding fathers, "that all men are created equal." A dream where EVERY American has the opportunity to live, grow up and be the person they were intended to be. A dream where every American has the opportunity to develop their own character so that, in the words of King, they may be judged "by the content of their character."

The time has come to **CHANGE THE SHAME**. The time has come to end ABORTION.

GROUP DISCUSSION— *I Have A Dream*

How do you think it is possible for the U.S. Supreme Court to have made such poor decisions in the Dred Scott and Plessy cases?

(For Men) If you were an adult in the 1920 era, how do you think you would have voted on allowing women the right to vote? Why?

(For Women) If you were an adult in the 1920 era, what action would you have been willing to take to procure the right to vote?

What do you think about the Author's claim that the primary responsibility of the government is to protect the Civil Rights of each citizen?

What do you think is the appropriate response when the government fails to protect the Civil Rights of a class of citizens?

If you skipped watching the Martin Luther King Jr speech, your assignment is to go back and watch it. Is there a point in his speech that resonates more strongly with you? If so, which point?

For the first time the Author discloses that abortion is the topic of this book; how do you feel about the Author's implication that taking the life of an unborn child through abortion is a violation of the child's fundamental Right to Life? _____

_____

_____

_____

_____

_____

Read Micah 6:8. Here we read a summary of what God requires from His people; how do you think abortion fits into His requirement to "act justly"? _____

_____

_____

_____

_____

_____

CHAPTER THREE

A Movement No Longer

"Too often...we enjoy the comfort of opinion without the discomfort of thought."

—John F. Kennedy

A Second Civil War sounds so messy, couldn't we cure this injustice with a nice happy "Movement" where everyone plays nice and nobody gets hurt?

Let's look again at history for a moment. Slavery was abolished in France in 1795, re-established by Napoleon in 1802, and abolished again in 1848. Slavery was abolished throughout the British Empire in 1833. The American Slavery Abolition Movement can trace its roots back to the 1770's. This American Abolition Movement saw huge number gains in the late 1820's and early 1830's, so by 1838 the American Anti-Slavery Society had 1350 local chapters with around 250,000 members.

By the time the American Civil War broke out in 1861, the Abolition Movement and the idea to abolish slavery had been around for at least ninety years. But despite the huge gains in numbers, they were no closer to seeing the end of slavery in the United States than they had been in 1804 when New Jersey was the last northern state to abolish it. For the dedicated abolitionist that was almost sixty years of frustration where the Abolition Movement saw little, if any, progress. Four years of Civil War did what ninety years of a "Movement" could not.

The Pro-life Movement has been active for more than forty years. Compare that to a couple of other, more successful movements. While the Women's Suffrage Movement had been around for many years it really didn't get much traction until 1913. Seven years later, in 1920, women were granted the right to vote. The Civil Rights Movement is considered to have started about the time of Rosa Park's refusal to give up her seat in 1955. Nine years later the Civil Rights Act of 1964 was passed.

A successful "movement" seems to get the job done in just a few years. But after forty years the Pro-life Movement is no closer to ending abortion than the Slavery Abolitionist Movement was to ending slavery after its last sixty years (1805-1865). **It took a Civil War to end slavery and it will take a Second Civil War to end abortion.**

There was a statement in the Introduction of this book and it is not only worthy of repeating but requires repeating:

> *This Second Civil War will NOT be fought on battlefields or with guns and canons. Those fighting against this injustice must do so WITHOUT violence, the taking of lives, or the destruction of property. This Second Civil War will be fought in the marketplace, in the polls and in the hearts and minds of the American people. The First Civil War needed bullets and bayonets; the Second Civil war will be fought with dollars and votes.*

Let's be painfully clear. NO VIOLENCE. Those wingnuts who want to shoot abortionists or bomb abortion clinics only HURT the cause and provide the abortion-friendly media with the fodder necessary to label all Pro-justice people a bunch of terrorists and nut cases. If this war is to be fought and won in the hearts and minds of the American people it must be accomplished through logic, financial pressure, political pressure, and honorable actions. It's not that we don't intend to inflict pain, but it's how we inflict this pain that matters.

Many Americans are apathetic about abortion so violence will only serve to drive them into the enemy's camp. You will see later that this war can be won with the right application of your votes and where you spend your dollars. The key is to win the apathetic; let's briefly visit that topic.

On a scale of 1-10 how would you rate your position on abortion?

1 ___ 2 ___ 3 ___ 4 ___ 5 ___ 6 ___ 7 ___ 8 ___ 9 ___ 10
Strongly Pro-abortion   Neutral   Strongly Pro-justice

If we are honest, most of us would probably be closer to neutral than we would be to either of the extremes. Approximately 35% of Americans aged 20-60 have been involved in an abortion. Of those who have not, most know someone close to them who has experienced one. Many experience guilt over their abortion involvement in varying degrees of frequency and intensity while others have put their abortion experience behind them and rarely, if ever, think of it.

Unless you were a slave held in bondage, pre-Civil War Americans generally gave very little thought to the plight of those millions of slaves held in captivity. The unjust treatment of the unborn is no different. Even with the widespread effect that abortion has had on most Americans it is probably safe to say that, for the majority of Americans, the injustice of abortion consumes very little of our daily thoughts or concerns.

The apathy toward slavery started changing among the masses with John Brown's raid on Harpers Ferry. As the nation endured four years of Civil War, slavery and the effects of the war soon became the primary focus of the news media and private conversations. It took the Civil War for most people to get off their apathy and give serious thought to the evils and the injustice of slavery.

As more and more Americans become seriously committed to defending the Civil Rights of the unborn, the effects of their honorable actions cannot help but be noticed by the media and the apathetic.

A Second Civil War seems rather harsh; what is meant by that? A Second Civil War means a total shift in strategy. For forty years well-meaning "Pro-life" people, through their support of Pregnancy Resource Centers, have been offering a variety of services to women (and men) facing an unplanned pregnancy. These services include:

▸ Crisis Pregnancy Counseling

▸ Free Pregnancy Tests

▸ Free Ultra-sounds

▸ STD Testing

▸ Providing Diapers and other Baby Supplies

▸ Providing Maternity Clothes

▸ Adoption Services

▸ Post-abortion Counseling

While these things are all necessary and do a great deal of good it's time to realize that these activities and services alone will never bring an end to abortion.

Dr. Day Gardner, President of National Black Pro-life Union, is nationally known for her work in exposing the abortion industry's exploitation of Black Americans through the placement of abortion clinics in black neighborhoods and their marketing strategies targeting young black women.

In a radio interview on February 18, 2013, Gardner was asked if she felt she was making inroads in the Black Community on this particular issue, especially when the evidence is so overwhelming that Blacks are being targeted. "No, I don't," Gardner replied. To her credit, Gardner quickly rebounded, but the frustration in her voice while responding to this question is undeniable. Gardner's refreshingly honest response poignantly illustrates the building frustration caused by the lack of meaningful progress in the 40+ year old Pro-life Movement.

The abortion industry is no longer threatened by the Pro-life Movement. The abortion industry has portrayed Pregnancy Resource Centers as a bunch of old fashioned grannies sitting around in rocking chairs knitting baby booties while waiting on some pregnant, unwed woman to walk through the doors. Once their victim arrives, the grannies turn into a gang of angry religious zealots who pounce on this unsuspecting woman until they have worn her down. She will not be allowed to leave the premises until she has found Jesus and promises to carry her baby full-term.

Unfortunately, in some cases, the abortion industry's portrayal of Pregnancy Resource Centers isn't too far off. I'm certainly not criticizing the heart or motives of those who, for the past 40+ years, have given so very much to defend the Civil Rights of the unborn. All I'm saying is that we need a change in tactics. A "Movement" isn't cutting it. We need a plan that will rock our nation. We need to put the abortion industry out of business.

The time has come to **CHANGE THE SHAME** and to Change the Shame we will need a Second Civil War.

GROUP DISCUSSION— *A Movement No Longer*

What are your thoughts regarding the Author's claim that ending abortion will take a Second Civil War?

On the scale of 1-10, where did you rate your position on abortion?

How often would you guess that the subject of abortion enters your thoughts?

Is there a Pregnancy Resource Center near where you live?

If so, have you ever been involved with it?

What do you think about the Author's claim that young black women are the target of the abortion industry?

Read Psalm 139. Verses 13-16 talk about God's plan for us while we are still in the womb. What relevance do you think that this passage has to the abortion debate today?

What do you think needs to happen to bring an end to abortion?

CHAPTER FOUR
Shame, What Shame?

"Do not withhold good from those who deserve it, when it is in your power to act."

—King Solomon

What is meant by this statement made at the conclusion of the previous chapter, "The time has come to **CHANGE THE SHAME**"?

Let's start by discussing what is NOT meant by this statement.

This statement is not meant to condemn, judge or embarrass any woman who has had an abortion, nor any boyfriend, husband, friend or parent that has played a role in a woman having an abortion. All members of mankind have done things that are wrong, have mistreated others and have done things they are ashamed of. None of us can change what has happened in the past. What we *can do* is learn from our mistakes, find healing, offer forgiveness and change the future.

We all have a moral compass placed within us, and we all know that the killing of another innocent human being is wrong. As a nation, we are appalled and deeply saddened when we see innocent school children slaughtered as a result of a "choice" made by some deranged individual. But why are we shocked? For 40+ years we have been saying that killing children is okay. By our actions or our silence we have participated in allowing a culture to develop that does not value human life. And then we wonder how these deranged people could ever commit such a hideous act?

Over a million innocent unborn children are slaughtered every year in the U.S. But this doesn't seem to bother most of us because, as a nation, we have chosen to believe the abortion industry's lie that a "choice" is more important than a life and that convenience is more important than justice.

Modern science and medicine provide overwhelming evidence that life begins at conception. In other words, the unborn child is a human being. Any argument that continues to challenge this fact is as intellectually dishonest as the claim of Pro-slavery advocates that "Negro" slaves were not human beings.

Because the evidence that life begins at conception is so overwhelming, most outspoken defenders of abortion will no longer argue this position because they would risk looking foolish and the loss of credibility. This matter has been so thoroughly presented in other books that I will not rehash it in this one other than to make the next couple of statements:

Life begins at conception and with that life comes certain Human and Civil Rights that we are all entitled to.

If we were to be truthful with ourselves we know that "*LIFE FOUND ON MARS*" would be the headlines if any life was found on Mars that possessed features of development similar to the life found in a one day old human embryo.

Millions of women regret their abortion and say they would not have had one had they felt they had a better option. Generally, women do not want to have abortions. But they have been told that abortion is the lesser of two evils and that, through some sort of twisted logic, they are actually doing their baby a favor by ending its life. In their time of "crisis" they are being taken advantage of by an abortion industry that has learned to capitalize on our culture which worships the god of convenience.

We are all responsible for our actions and passing the blame for our decisions onto a friend, parent, boyfriend, counselor or the abortion industry will only work for a while. Sooner or later we must all face the reality of our choices and must take responsibility for them.

Many women who have experienced an abortion medicate their feelings of guilt and shame with excessive eating, drugs, alcohol, promiscuity, work or activism— maybe even Pro-life activism. Many women are so ashamed of their abortion that they have never mentioned it to family, close friends or even their spouse. Men tend to talk about their abortion involvement even less.

If you have experienced an abortion please check out the resources on our website at *ChangeTheShame.com* or visit a chapter of Abortion Anonymous; their information can be found at *AbAnon.org*.

While men and women who have experienced abortions may struggle with personal shame, the purpose of this book is not to inflict additional personal shame on any of these individuals. Rather, the purpose of this book is to expose the shame of our nation and our leadership, and more importantly, to change the shame by ending abortion within this nation.

So, let's discuss *shame*; how are we guilty of shameful attitudes and actions?

First, **Shame on Me**. It has taken far too long for me to write this book and to do what I can to bring an end to the injustice of abortion. I have been aware of this injustice for thirty years. Sure, I've given money, volunteered where I could and even served on a Pregnancy Resource Center Board for several years. But honestly, I've been more concerned about my life and my business than I have been with justice and saving the lives of unborn children.

If I were to witness someone being randomly attacked I'm confident that I would rush to their defense. But when it comes to abortion I've been like the cowardly bystander, watching from a distance, cheering on those brave enough to get involved. I've been more concerned over what others might think, or how focused involvement might affect my business. I have been unwilling to fully commit myself to ending this shameful injustice.

I am no longer standing on the sidelines; I'm now a fully committed player on the field. As long as I have breath I will do whatever I'm able to end abortion, especially throughout the United States.

Next, **Shame on our Nation**. As a nation we have imposed economic sanctions against foreign countries for their unacceptable record on Human Rights issues. We've overthrown dictators because of their practice of genocide. Talk about hypocrisy! How would our nation respond if another country decided to impose economic sanctions against us for our Human Rights record against the unborn? No nation on this planet has taken human life through genocide in numbers remotely close to the number of lives our nation has taken through abortion.

Think about it! What if a commando squad from another country made an attempt to remove a sitting president because of his or her genocidal position on abortion? Of course this sounds absurd but we, as a nation, are just as guilty of these infractions as are other nations. While I agree that wherever and whenever we have the opportunity to end violations of Human Rights, our nation should act. But we should get our Human Rights house in order before we hypocritically start throwing our weight around to correct injustices elsewhere.

As I mentioned earlier, we have participated in creating a culture that does not value human life, yet we are rightfully shocked and appalled when a gunman storms into a school and slaughters innocent children. Why can't we connect the dots? If we teach our children that life means nothing by condoning the slaughter of innocent babies….if we misdirect their moral compass….why are we so shocked when they act in a manner consistent with what they've been taught?

Shame on the U.S. Supreme Court. Many believe the worst decision ever made by the U.S. Supreme Court came in the Dred Scott Decision of 1857, which affirmed the right to own slaves. As I alluded to earlier, that decision was not the worst decision the U.S. Supreme Court has ever made. The biggest blunder in the history of the U.S. Supreme Court was the 1973 ruling in Roe v. Wade. In this case the U.S. Supreme Court ruled that a Right to privacy under the Due Process Clause of the Fourteenth Amendment extended to a woman's decision regarding an abortion. This rationale is absolutely absurd.

If you recall, the Fourteenth Amendment is the Amendment that gave U.S. citizenship to all those born in the United States. It was ratified in 1868, just three years after the Civil War and 105 years before the Roe v. Wade decision. At that time some states and local governments were passing laws that limited the freedoms of the newly freed "Negro" slaves; corrective action was needed to protect the Rights of these former slaves so the Fourteenth Amendment was passed.

The Due Process Clause of the Fourteenth Amendment prohibits state and local governments from depriving persons of life, liberty, or property without certain protective measures being taken to ensure fairness. The Due Process Clause offered citizens protection from unjust treatment or killing by those in power. This Clause was included to protect life and freedoms, not take them.

It's horrifically ironic that by taking the Due Process Clause of the Fourteenth Amendment out of its historical context, the very clause that was intended to protect life and Human Rights is used as justification to destroy life and deny Human Rights.

In the same way that we needed to remedy or overturn the Dred Scott and other debacles of the U.S. Supreme Court, so we need to overturn the decision of Roe v. Wade.

Shame on the U.S. President. When it comes to protecting the Civil Rights of the unborn, the current President, Barack Obama, has the worst record of any

President. As an Illinois State Senator and a U.S. Senator he consistently voted against Civil Rights for the Unborn. While campaigning in 2008, Obama used the wording that his daughters should not be "punished with a baby" if they made a mistake in their sexual activity.

In addressing the nation after the terrible and tragic Sandy Hook Elementary shootings, Obama stated that each time he hears of one of these shootings he reacts, "not as president but as a parent." He goes on to say that the majority of those who died were children between five and ten years old.

When watching this live broadcast I remember saying out loud to those in the room, "What a hypocrite! He (Obama) can get all emotional over a tragic shooting of innocent children but he has no problem with killing the unborn. There is no difference; both are equally tragic."

As you read the following Obama comments, think of them not only in the context of Sandy Hook, but also in the context of the injustice to the unborn through abortion.

> *"They had their entire lives ahead of them, birthdays, graduations, weddings, kids of their own."*
>
> *"So our hearts are broken today."*
>
> *"As a country we have been through this too many times. We're going to have to come*

together and take meaningful action to prevent more tragedies like this, regardless of the politics."

This video of Obama can be seen at *http://www.youtube. com/watch?v=q_8zXJcoxHY.*

You can use this QR code to view this video from your mobile device:

Get the free mobile app at
http://gettag.mobi

Shame on the Democratic Party.
The Democratic Party represents itself as being the champion of the little guy. It's the party that looks out for minorities, workers and the disenfranchised, protecting them from being trampled on by what they portray as "heartless" employers and "greedy" corporations. Yet their election campaigns are financed by businesses that support the abortion industry, the biggest corporate villains of all.

Because the unborn have *no voice* and *no vote* they need a party to stand up for their rights more so than any other demographic. Those leading the Democratic Party are hypocrites; if they truly were the champion of the little guy they would be standing up for the Civil Rights of the unborn. I applaud the few Democrats who see abortion for the injustice that it is; do not remain silent when you have the opportunity to influence others within your party.

Shame on the Republican Party. Unlike the Democratic Party, the Republican Party does not boast in being the champion for the rights of the little guy, but I believe the hypocrisy of the Republican Party to be equal to that of the Democratic Party. The Republican Party claims to be Pro-life, a claim that appears as mere window dressing to gain the political favor of Pro-life voters. While I believe there are many Republicans truly opposed to the injustice of abortion, very few are willing to defend the unborn to the extent that it would jeopardize their political careers. If the Republican Party was as committed to ending the injustice of abortion as they are to their re-election, abortion in our nation would have ended years ago.

Shame on the Mainstream News Media. The following is a quote from *USAWatchdog.com* 8/23/2010.

> *Recently, a new Gallup poll delivered some bad news to mainstream media– only one fourth of people asked believe what it says. The Gallup story said, "Americans continue to express near-record-low confidence in newspapers and television news– with no more than 25% of Americans saying they have a "great deal" or "quite a lot" of confidence in either.*

With newspapermen like abolitionist William Lloyd Garrison, the media was influential in bringing an end to slavery. The media also played an important role in the Women's Suffrage and Civil Rights Movements. The news media used to stand for what is honorable and right.

But it seems that the mainstream news media has sold its soul and as the Gallup poll suggests, has lost its integrity along the way. Many in the media are puppets of special interest groups.

Mainstream news media has crucified many political candidates or public opinion leaders who have come out against abortion and in defense of justice for the unborn.

The media could once be trusted but that trust has been violated; without corrective action, their demise is certain. Americans will not pay attention to sources they do not trust. Advertising dollars are what fund the news and as these advertisers realize that the public trust is gone their advertising dollars will quickly disappear as well.

Shame on Religious and Church Leaders. During a conversation I had with a mid- twenty-year-old youth leader of a Junior High School church youth group, I asked him what he thought about abortion. He shrugged his shoulders, looked at me and said, "I don't know, never thought about it."

Abortion has been prevalent throughout the USA for two generations. One out of three women between the ages of twenty and sixty sitting in church pews today has had at least one abortion and with it tremendous emotional pain and anguish. Yet most preachers and religious leaders (an estimated 97%) say little or nothing about the matter and through their silence and apathy are putting a third generation at risk.

Just as with the Anti-slavery Movement prior to the Civil War, much of what has happened in the Pro-life Movement has come through the efforts of those within the Church. These well-meaning individuals have volunteered millions of hours and donated billions of dollars in an effort to bring justice to the unborn. But due to the apathy of church leadership, these faithful people represent only a very small percentage of the overall church population.

The end of abortion is nowhere in sight, and many of those involved with the "Pro-life Movement" have become weary or frustrated, content in the celebration of saving the occasional single life. I applaud you and celebrate with you, but it might be time to wake up and recognize that **IT AIN'T WORKING!** The reasons that the current strategy isn't working are:

1. There is no national comprehensive unified plan to end the injustice of abortion, and

2. Church and religious leaders are generally apathetic and therefore silent on the matter. By their silence they are sentencing another generation to be victims of the lies.

If church leadership made their churches a safe place where men and women could be honest and encouraged to tell their stories of the pain and sorrow abortion has caused, then abortion would end and the next generation rescued from the same pain and sorrow. If justice for the unborn became a priority for the majority (rather than just a few) of those within Church leadership, abortion would quickly end and The Church could get on with the business of healing and forgiving.

Shame on the Leaders of the Black Community. If there is any group of people within the United States that should understand the withholding of freedoms and the injustice that occurs when people are denied basic Civil Rights, it ought to be Black Americans. While there are many Black Americans who see abortion for the cruel injustice that it is, the vast majority of Blacks continue to support a political machine that has its foot on their throat— a political machine that encourages the killing of their unborn.

Most of those leading the Black community have failed to see the truth and as a result many Black Americans today live in political slavery, settling for the scraps that fall from their master's table.

Today Planned Parenthood targets Black and low income neighborhoods in which to place their abortion clinics. The freedom won through the Civil War and the rights recognized through the Civil Rights Movement can never be enjoyed by the Black baby never given a chance to be born.

More on this can be found at *http://www.nationalblackpro- lifeunion.com/.* You can use this QR code to view this website from your mobile device:

Get the free mobile app at
http://gettag.mobi

Changing the shame of our nation will only be done by:

1. Exposing the lies of the abortion industry.

2. Changing the awareness that abortion is a Civil Rights issue.

3. Dismantling the arguments used to defend this injustice.

4. Igniting a Second Civil War with the intent to bring this injustice to an end, and

5. Organizing millions of abortion abolitionists to create an "Underground Railroad" to serve the needs of women who find themselves in an unplanned pregnancy.

GROUP DISCUSSION— *Shame, What Shame?*

What do you think about the Author's claim that we should not be shocked when we hear of school shootings since we have allowed a culture of death to develop, a society that does not value human life?

In your opinion, when does life begin?

What is your opinion based on?

What do you think about the Author's claim that many women (and men) medicate their pain and shame of a past abortion through food, alcohol, drugs, work or activism?

66 | Change the Shame

The Author calls "Shame on" several groups, organizations and individuals. Which "shame on" do you most agree? ....

....

....

Is there a "Shame on" where you think the Author has gone too far? ....

....

....

What do you think about the Author calling President Obama a hypocrite? ....

....

....

....

Read Proverbs 3:21-35. Verse 27 tells us to not withhold good from those who deserve it when it is in your power to act. Do you believe that the unborn "deserve" good? If so, do you believe that you have the power to act on their behalf? And if so, in what ways do you have the power to act? ....

....

....

....

....

CHAPTER FIVE
Armed For Battle

"Better to remain silent and be thought a fool than to speak and to remove all doubt."

—Abraham Lincoln

Many consider abortion simply a moral issue and attempt to change the minds of others based on their own religious or spiritual point of view. While abortion is indeed a moral matter, it is pointless to attempt to change another person's opinion based on moral or religious grounds when that person has a different set of values or a different world view.

When defending the Civil Liberties of the unborn we must first find common ground with those we are attempting to persuade. Where are we in agreement and what values do we share in common? Without a common basis and belief in what is right or wrong any conversation about what is right or wrong is generally pointless. We cannot expect those with a different set of values to see things as we do. Understanding the values of those we are attempting to influence is the beginning of an effective conversation.

Too often the people who use the Bible as their moral compass try to use biblical values as a means to persuade another person that the other person's actions are inappropriate. But when the other person has no regard for biblical values or adheres to some other standard for moral guidance, preaching from the Bible will fall on deaf ears.

Here's a hint: the chances are very high that a young, pregnant, unwed, abortion-minded woman is NOT using the Bible as her moral compass. It's highly likely that any attempts to convince her that an abortion is wrong, based on what the Bible says, will be ineffective.

Furthermore, even when we know that something is wrong but desire to do it anyway, we tend to justify our actions until the wrong seems right in our own eyes. Most books written about abortion are approaching the topic from a moral or biblical point of view. In short, most of these books are preaching to the choir and their message is not getting through to those who need to hear it.

For this reason, this book presents abortion as a matter of justice rather than religion. Justice and fairness are things that we all understand and comprehend. We all can easily imagine the injustice of slavery and feel the torment of being the property of another.

We all can easily imagine the injustice experienced by Rosa Parks or Homer Plessy and how we would feel if we were told to surrender our bus seat or move to a different train car because we were the wrong color. We all can easily imagine how we would feel if we were forced to use an outdoor port-a-potty, while more affluent patrons of the same establishment were offered the use of luxurious indoor restrooms.

We all can easily imagine the embarrassment we would feel if we were seated in a restaurant and told in the presence of the other patrons that we must leave immediately because the owner didn't care to serve people confined to wheelchairs. We all can easily imagine the pain of injustice we would feel if the owner of the dream home we intended to purchase refused to sell to us because he didn't like the national origin of our grandparents.

A restaurant owner has the choice to refuse service to anyone, but should this right to choose trump the Civil Rights of another? A property owner has the choice to lease his property to whomever he desires, but should his right to choose trump the Civil Rights of someone else?

Is there any situation where a person is justified when making a choice that would trump the Civil Rights of another? Every American has the Right to Life, Liberty and the Pursuit of Happiness and the circumstances surrounding their conception should in no way diminish those Rights.

We should never be argumentative, condescending or emotional when talking to others who are Pro-abortion. If someone wants to have an honest, intelligent conversation then have one. But having an argument with someone who is unwilling to listen to an opposing point of view is a waste of time.

Ask questions to understand the views of others:

"If you were alive in the 1850's, which side of the slavery issue would you be on?" "Why?"

Based on the logic used by some today, it is easy to imagine someone alive in the 1850's saying, "I'm personally against slavery, but I feel that slavery is a private issue between the slave and their owner and is ultimately the slave-owner's "choice" whether they should free their slaves or not."

"If you had been alive during the women's suffrage movement, how would you feel about women having the right to vote?" "Why?"

Based on the logic used by some today, it is easy to imagine someone alive in the 1910's saying, "I'm personally in favor of granting women the Right to vote, but I feel that whether or not a woman has the intelligence to vote is a private matter between a woman and her husband and is ultimately the husband's "choice" whether or not his wife should vote."

"If you had been around during the Civil Rights Movement, what would have been your position on the equal treatment of all races?" "Why?"

Based on the logic used by some today, it is easy to imagine someone alive in the 1950's saying, "I'm personally against discrimination, but I feel that the choice of whom a business serves and the level of service they provide is a private issue for the business owner to decide based on a free market. Let the marketplace dictate how a business should operate rather than force businesses to serve customers they don't want. It should ultimately be the entrepreneur's "choice" whether they will treat all races equally or not."

"Is a person justified in the abusive treatment or in taking the life of someone else simply because that person has a physical or mental defect?" "Why?"

Based on the logic used by some today, it is easy to imagine someone saying, "I'm personally against abortion, but when the tests show that there is a strong possibility that a fetus is defective then the situation is different. I feel that terminating the pregnancy is a private matter between the doctor and the mother and is ultimately the mother's "choice" whether or not that child should live." Most Americans are appalled upon the hearing of the cruel or brutal treatment of a disabled individual. How then can we be so totally numb to the brutality conferred upon those within the womb simply because they have a disability?

If you lived in one of the many countries that give a husband the right to beat his wife, how would you feel about that? Can you imagine someone in the United States stating publicly that a man should have the right to beat his wife? How can anyone honestly think that abortion is any different?

With every conversation about abortion one question begs to be asked:

BUT, WHAT ABOUT THE BABY?

No matter how it's packaged, no matter how it's justified, no matter how it's glamorized, no matter how it's rationalized, no matter how vehemently defended: at the end of every abortion a baby is *dead*.

Abortion is such a hotly debated topic; the most outspoken on both sides are extremely passionate. Most Pro-choice extremists will never change their minds or their position any more than slave owners would give up their slaves 150 years ago. Pro-justice proponents will never change their minds or position any more than abolitionists would abandon their quest to free the slaves.

But I hope that anyone who is Pro-choice, with an open mind, will read these next few pages and consider that there is another, intellectually honest, position to consider.

If you are one who has given little or no thought to abortion, seeing it as somebody else's problem, please read the next few pages and consider how apathy can contribute to the injustice.

Perhaps you are an abortion abolitionist, who has heroically participated in this epic battle. Please take the time to educate yourself so you can defend your position intellectually and continue to do your part as this Second Civil War unfolds.

Put in its simplest terms, the battle over slavery boiled down to one thing: did the rights of the slaveowner trump another human being's Right to freedom? Slave owners believed that their right to own slaves trumped the inalienable Rights of the slaves. Abolitionists believed the inalienable Rights of the slaves trumped the rights of the slave-owner.

Similarly, the battle over abortion boils down to one thing: does the woman's right to choose trump the Civil Rights of the baby? Pro-abortionists think that a woman's right to "choose" trump the baby's Civil Rights. Pro-justice advocates think that the Civil Rights of the baby trump the woman's rights to "choose."

Historically, this nation has eventually found its way to the fundamental truth that any lesser right a person might possess yields to the greater Civil Rights, the Rights of *Life, Liberty and the Pursuit of Happiness.* In other words, rights are no longer rights when they trample on the Civil Liberties of another. But for over forty years, we have allowed a lesser right (a woman's choice) to trump the greater Civil Rights of her unborn child.

So when it comes to a woman's body (or anyone's for that matter) her rights are undeniable. She may wear whatever she likes, eat whatever she likes, cut her hair however she likes, pierce and paint her body however she likes, exercise as little or as much as she likes, drink whatever she likes, educate herself however she wishes and pursue whatever dreams she likes. But a woman's right to do whatever she wants to do with and to her body is *trumped* by the Right of her unborn child to *LIFE*.

Looking back, arguments used by defenders of slavery seem absurd. These arguments are presented in detail on a variety of websites including:

http://www.ushistory.org/us/27f.asp

http://abolition.e2bn.org/slavery_112.html

http://www.studymode.com/essays/Southern-Arguments-Slavery-50829.html

If we are to change two generations of abortion shame by changing the hearts and minds of the American people, we better know what we are talking about. The objective of this chapter is to equip the reader with the tools necessary to expose the intellectual dishonesty of the arguments used in defense of the injustice of abortion. **Ironically, the arguments used in defense of abortion are the very same arguments that were used in the defense of slavery over a century and a half ago.**

COMPARE THE ARGUMENTS:

Argument for Slavery: **"The Negro slave is not a human, or, at best, an inferior race and therefore does not have the civil liberties due to white men."** This was the principal argument used by those who defended slavery prior to the Civil War and was given further validity with the Dred Scott Decision.

Argument for Abortion: **"The unborn child is not yet human and therefore does not have the civil liberties due to those who have been born."** Proponents of abortion use the "unborn are not human" as their principal argument in the defense of abortion. This argument is just as absurd today as the "Negro is not human" defense was back then. Any self-respecting, intellectually honest scientist or medical professional will contend that human life begins at conception. The scientific evidence supporting this position is overwhelming and indisputable.

Consider this quote from Randy Alcorn:

> *"At conception the embryo begins new life which develops into a fetus. Fetus does not mean "non-human;" fetus is Latin meaning "offspring," "young one" or "little child." Like the term "baby," "toddler," "child," or "adolescent," the term fetus refers to a particular stage of human development. The four differences between the born and unborn are: size, level of development, environment*

and degree of dependency; all of these differences continue for many years after the birth of the child."[1]

Argument for Slavery: **"Slaves are my personal property; neither the government nor anyone else has any business telling me how I ought to treat them."** Slave-owners argued that their ownership rights trumped those of their slaves. Not only was slavery itself an injustice, but in some cases slave owners killed or denied care to a slave because the slave was too old or sick and was deemed no longer useful.

On January 1, 1863, President Abraham Lincoln issued the Emancipation Proclamation freeing all slaves and declaring them persons with rights and representation by the U.S. government. He delivered the Emancipation Proclamation as "an act of justice."

Argument for Abortion: **"The unborn child is part of the woman's body and a personal health issue; neither the government nor anyone else has any business telling a woman what she can or cannot do with her body."** In the same manner as with slave-owners, the woman's rights are said to trump those of her unborn child. We have repeatedly established that individual rights are never to trump the Civil Liberties of another. Yet, with reference to unborn children, we continue the injustice of denying them their Rights in the most extreme way possible—by terminating their lives.

Argument for Slavery: **"The Negro, as a slave, will have a better quality of life."** Many slave owners justified slavery by taking the position that the Negro did not have the intelligence necessary to survive and that their lives were much better off as slaves. Today we know that given the opportunity and education, members of any race are able to accomplish anything they set their minds to do.

Argument for Abortion: **"The baby, if left to live, will not have a meaningful quality of life."** This is the argument used to justify elimination of the unwanted, disabled or otherwise disadvantaged child and is equally unjust. Disabled individuals are just as much a part of our community as any demographic and make enormous contributions to society.

Many people become handicapped or disabled as children or adults. Should we euthanize them because "they will not have a meaningful quality of life?" Imagine the parents of a ten-year-old boy learning that their son has just been in an accident and will no longer have his sight. Or imagine a case where parents became extremely frustrated over having to care for their disabled three-year-old. We would be outraged if an attempt was made to pass a law that would allow parents to take their child's life in cases like these.

The real issue is not about the meaningfulness or quality of the unborn *child's* life. The real issue and justification for the killing the unborn with disabilities is about the quality of the *parents'* lives, just as the real issue for slave owners was the quality of their own lives. If someone doesn't want to parent and care for a disabled child, then fine, there is no shame in that. Give the child to someone who will love and care for them; millions of parents would gladly take them and love them as their own.

Argument for Slavery: **"Slaves are necessary as a matter of economy and convenience; it's a matter of quality of life or standard of living."** Slave owners argued that slavery was a necessary building block of both the national and individual economy and to do away with slavery would severely damage both. Basically, all arguments defending slavery were based on the rationale that money, pleasure or personal convenience of the slave-owner was more important than the life and freedom of the slave.

Argument for Abortion: **"An unplanned pregnancy interferes with my education, career plans, or personal financial plans; basically, it's a matter of quality of life or standard of living."** What would we think of a man who killed his children because he had lost his job and could no longer afford to provide for them? What would we think about a father who decided to kill his children because he wanted to further his education or return to the party life of his youth and didn't want the burden or responsibility of caring for offspring? We would be outraged if parents killed their toddlers using the same reasoning as parents use to kill their unborn children.

It is intellectually dishonest to think that killing the unborn for a monetary or personal convenience reason is justified. The Civil Rights of the unborn should be defended as ardently as the Civil Rights of any child.

Argument for Slavery: **"Since slavery is legal, I'm not doing anything wrong."** Not only was slavery legal in the laws of many States, slavery was further sanctioned by the Supreme Court in the infamous Dred Scott Decision. Although legal, slavery was later abolished as people began to see it for the injustice that it truly was. But even after slavery was abolished, it took another one hundred years for Black Americans and other minorities to be granted, within the law, the same rights granted to all others by the U.S. Constitution. As slavery has taught us, making something legal does not make it right!

Argument for Abortion: **"Since Abortion is legal, I'm not doing anything wrong."** Not only was abortion legal in many States, abortion was further sanctioned and made the law of the land by the Supreme Court in the Roe v. Wade decision. Just as it took brave individuals willing to fight the injustice of slavery, it will take many brave individuals willing to do the same for the unborn. All of us have someone to thank for the Freedoms and the Civil Rights we enjoy today; it is our responsibility to do the same for future generations and not give up until the day that Roe v. Wade has been overturned and abortion has been abolished.

Argument for Slavery: **"I'm a benevolent slave owner; if my slaves were owned by someone else they would be abused."** This argument takes a similar position as the "Quality of Life" argument. In other words, "My justification as a slave owner is that I'm preventing *slave abuse.*"

Argument for Abortion: **"Out of a sense of benevolence, we should abort children to prevent child abuse."** Some argue that an unwanted child, if left to live, would be born to parents who might abuse the child. Hence, they argue that it is better to *kill* the child rather than unnecessarily subject that child to possible abuse. But abortion is *the ultimate child abuse!* Would there not be public outrage if the Child Protective Agency in your State decided to kill abused children to protect them from further abuse?

Argument for Slavery: **"The Negro born of free parents is free; the Negro born of slave parents is a slave."** Those defending slavery argued that the circumstances of conception dictated the freedoms due the individual. The owner of cattle is owner of the cattle's offspring and just as with cattle; the owner of the slave is owner of the slave's offspring. In other words, they argued that a person's rights to freedom were dependent upon their status at birth.

Argument for Abortion: **"Abortion is justified in circumstances of rape or incest."** This position mirrors the slavery position that the circumstances of conception dictated the rights due an individual. **"Should a woman be forced to carry a child conceived in rape?"** This rhetorical question has been a stumbling point for many well-meaning defenders of justice for the unborn. Anyone answering this question in the affirmative appears heartless, insensitive and cruel.

The true question is this: **Should the circumstances of one's conception diminish or nullify one's Civil Liberties**? If the act of rape or how one is conceived establishes an individual's Rights then the thirty-year-old man conceived in rape should have Rights inferior to the thirty-year-old man conceived in love. Would it be okay to deny an individual conceived in rape the Right to vote or to eat in a restaurant of their choice?

In the tragic event of a rape, for justice to be served, it may indeed be true that a life should be taken, but justice is not served by taking the life of the innocent. If justice demands the taking of life then justice is served by taking the life of the guilty, the rapist. The violence conferred upon the rape victim is in no way diminished by conferring that same violence upon the baby through the injustice of an abortion.

OTHER THOUGHTS REGARDING SLAVERY AND ABORTION

Let's say a slave owner rapes one of his slave girls and she becomes pregnant. Should the child born of this tragic union be slave or free? Who today would say that this child should be a slave? Yet, wouldn't it be hypocritical for someone to defend abortion while holding to the opinion that the child should be free? One might say that the child has no Rights and should be killed or made a slave, but to say that the child should be free is to assume the child has *Civil Rights*. The Right to *freedom* is great; the Right to *life* is even greater.

Those defending abortion would have you believe that **terminating an unwanted pregnancy is no different than the removal of a wart or tumor.** Warts and tumors, if left alone, don't grow to be mature human beings. However, if left alone, a fetus will grow into an infant then on to maturity. Whether one day, one month, fully grown or in the latter months of old age, the Civil Rights and Liberties of all human beings deserve protection.

Consider this: friends and family mourn with the parents who have lost a baby due to miscarriage. Why is it that no thought or concern is ever expressed to the parents of a child lost through an abortion? Millions of women suffer with Post-abortive Syndrome; the pain and guilt are very real. Proponents of abortion deny this pain exists. Parents need to mourn and be comforted over the loss of any child regardless of the circumstances of the child's death.

Just as our nation needed healing following the Civil War, so our nation will need healing when abortion is abolished. Men and women who have participated in abortions should not be condemned or judged, for we all have been deceived and have made mistakes at one time or another. A safe and confidential place to find abortion healing is through Abortion Anonymous. (*www.abanon.org*)

Looking back, we see clearly how absurd and intellectually dishonest were the arguments used to defend slavery. These very same arguments are equally absurd and intellectually dishonest when used in the defense of abortion today.

Abortion MUST and WILL be abolished in the United States because, at the end of the day, abortion, just like slavery, denies another human being their Right to LIFE, LIBERTY and the pursuit of HAPPINESS. Just as others have made great sacrifices to secure our Rights and freedoms, it is our responsibility to do the same for future generations.

Endnotes

1   Randy Alcorn, *Why Pro-life?* (Peabody, MA: Hendrickson Publishers, 2004), p. 31.

GROUP DISCUSSION— *Armed for Battle*

The Author states that most Pro-Life books are written from the point of view that abortion is a moral or religious issue; what do you think about the Author's claim that abortion must be ended as a matter of justice?

Imagine a young couple thrilled and excited to learn that they are expecting a child. After a few weeks pass, this same excited couple learns that their unborn child may have Down Syndrome or some other disability so they are considering aborting their child. This couple wants your advice; what would you tell them?

In your opinion, taking the life of an unborn child is justified in what situations?

In your opinion, taking the life of a one-year old toddler is justified in what situations?

Is there any difference in your previous two answers?

If so, why?

The Author claims that the arguments used to defend slavery are the same arguments used to defend abortion. Do you agree? Why or why not?

The fallback position of pro-abortionists in every debate is the question of rape; it is their last line of defense. The Author's position is to reword the question, "Should the circumstances of one's conception diminish or nullify one's Civil Liberties?" What are your thoughts?

Read Deuteronomy 21:1-9. The people of Israel were commander to complete this extensive process whenever there was the shedding of innocent blood and it was unknown who had slain the innocent party. This was done lest the blood of the innocent person be on the hands of the elders of the nearest town. In what way do you think this passage reflects the heart of God when it comes to the shedding of innocent blood and the responsibility of those in leadership to protect the innocent?

CHAPTER SIX
The Underground Railroad

"When a man steals to satisfy hunger, we may safely conclude that there is something wrong in society—so when a woman destroys the life of her unborn child, it is an evidence that either by education or circumstances she has been greatly wronged."

—**Mattie Brinkerhoff,**
***The Revolution*, September 2, 1869**

Prior to the Civil War efforts were made by slave abolitionists to free as many slaves as possible. One example is Harriet Tubman. She is credited with freeing seventy slaves through what was known as the "Underground Railroad." Tubman had been a slave herself, but after she secured her freedom she became determined to secure the freedom for the rest of her family. Once she started there was no stopping her. She knew that if she were caught she could be forced back into slavery or possibly killed. Today she is memorialized for the true hero she was; she placed the freedom of others above her own life.

Through the Underground Railroad slaves would get word to run away from their masters and to be at a specific place at a specific time. If a run-away slave was caught, it was certain that they would be badly beaten if not killed; slave-owners believed that examples had to be made of slaves attempting to runaway to keep the rest of the slaves from attempting the same thing. Once the slave ran away he or she trusted their lives totally into the hands of strangers. These abolitionist strangers would provide food, clothing, shelter and transportation. The run-away slaves were often handed from stranger to stranger while traveling hundreds of miles in their journey to safety. Many were taken all the way to Canada.

These Underground Railroad abolitionists sacrificed much for slaves while knowing they probably would never see these slaves again. They risked punishment while spending their time and money for those that could never repay this incredible debt. Even with all that was involved in freeing a slave, freedom was only the beginning. Once the run-away slave had secured their freedom there was still the need to house, educate, train, find employment and transition the former slave into a completely different culture. What good is it to free a man from slavery only to have him die of exposure or starvation?

Ending abortion is necessary to protect the Civil Rights of the unborn, but we must understand that ending abortion is only a small part of the work that needs to be done. Caring for the needs of the baby and the mother (or parents) is just as vital as protecting the Civil Rights of the unborn. It is not enough to say to a woman, "Don't have an abortion and here are the reasons why…." As Pro-justice advocates we must be committed to meeting the physical, financial, emotional, educational and spiritual needs of both baby and mother (parents).

Just as a the Underground Railroad was needed with the first Civil War, so another Underground Railroad is needed as we embark on the Second Civil War. Millions of abolitionist recruits are needed for this new Underground Railroad. This army of recruits will need leaders, planners, organizers, administrators, speakers/communicators, marketing experts, website developers, social media users, lawyers, accountants, mechanics, handymen, people with sales skills, people who understand politics, teachers, stay-at-home moms, coaches, youth workers and on and on. In this army there is a place for anyone and everyone who cares about justice.

This Underground Railroad will need some structure and organization on a national level, but will mostly be a grass roots effort planned and implemented at the local level. This Underground Railroad will include many of the services that Pregnancy Resource Centers have been offering for years, but as the unborn are finally recognized as having *protected Rights* and Roe v. Wade is finally overturned, these services will shift from saving lives and providing for the unborn to exclusively providing services for women who find themselves in an unplanned pregnancy.

Many Pregnancy Resource Centers are already providing some of these and other services to women in an unplanned pregnancy. Here is a list of services Pregnancy Resource Centers may want to consider adding, expanding or outsourcing:

▶ Adoption Services

▶ Pregnancy Testing

▶ Legal Services

▶ Providing Infant Food and Clothing

▶ Providing Maternity Clothing

▶ Parental Training and Mentorship

▶ Pre-Marital Counseling

▶ Relationship Mentoring

▶ Childcare Services

▶ Public Assistance Counseling

▶ Financial Management Counseling

▶ Financial Assistance Programs

▶ Spiritual Mentorship/Partnership

▶ Godparent Sponsorships

▸ Adopt-A-Mother Programs

▸ Educational Scholarships and Tutoring

▸ Job Training and Placement Services

▸ Public Assistance Counseling

▸ Foster Parenting for Mother and Child

Basically, Pregnancy Resource Centers will realize that they are not only needed in the moment of crisis, but that their greatest opportunity is in meeting the needs of their clients beyond the crisis. The most effective way to end abortion is by eliminating the reasons that women feel they need to have an abortion. We must put actions to our words by embracing the following philosophical positions:

1. If we are encouraging women to carry their child full term then we need to do everything in our power to eliminate the reasons that cause women to feel that abortion is their most attractive option. This will only happen if women know that the needs of mother and child will be met throughout her pregnancy and beyond.

2. If a woman makes a heroic choice to place her child for adoption we need to have the systems in place to make adoption a positive experience for all involved and to honor the mother for making this choice.

3. If a woman makes the choice to raise her child, with or without the father, we need to make

certain that this woman and her child have access to whatever resources are reasonably needed to give them a fair chance at happiness.

Can we meet every need of every woman? Of course not. Will some women abuse the programs and services? Probably. Once a woman has become pregnant, whether they have an abortion, raise the child or place it for adoption, their life will never be the same. Whatever their choice, life will be significantly harder and forever changed. Empowering and equipping them to deal with and work through these changes will become the objective.

Abortion has been around since recorded history. According to George Grant in his book *"Third Time Around"*:

> *"Virtually every culture in antiquity was stained with the blood of innocent children. Unwanted infants in ancient Rome were abandoned outside the city walls to die from exposure to the elements or from attacks of wild foraging beasts. Greeks often gave their pregnant women harsh doses of herbal or medicinal abortifacients. Persians developed highly sophisticated surgical curette procedures. Chinese women tied heavy ropes around their waists so excruciatingly tight that they either aborted or*

> *passed into unconsciousness. Ancient Hindus and Arabs concocted chemical pessaries-abortifacients that were pushed or pumped directly into the womb through the birth canal. Primitive Canaanites threw their children onto flaming pyres as a sacrifice to their god Molech. Polynesians subjected their pregnant women to onerous tortures-their abdomens beaten with large stones or hot coals heaped upon their bodies. Japanese women straddled boiling cauldrons of parricidal brews. Egyptians disposed of their unwanted children by disemboweling and dismembering them shortly after birth-their collagen was then ritually harvested for the manufacture of cosmetic creams."*[2]

Since the time of Christ, Christians have historically been the ones defending the Rights of the unborn. While many of those within the Pro-life community today consider themselves Christians, the Christian community as a whole has largely abandoned their historical role of defending the Rights of the unborn. In other words, in recent years, most Christian churches and organized religion have done *very little* in defending the Rights of the unborn.

Churches have relegated their role to one that is merely supportive, occasionally throwing a financial bone in the direction of the local Pregnancy Resource Center or allowing some Pro-life organization to show a five minute video each year on National Right-to-Life Sunday. It is only a few members of these churches that have been doing all the heavy lifting in the effort to protect the unborn these past 40+ years. There are a few exceptions, most notably the Catholic Church.

Starting in 1930, several Christian Denominations actually came out with statements defending abortion. Most of these statements have since been recanted, but it's hard to imagine that the Christian community could be as numb about abortion as many in the church had been about slavery before the Civil War. There are many things that could potentially cause disunity among the Christian community, but abortion should not be one of them. Defending the Rights of the unborn should be a cause that brings the Christian community together in unity.

The following is taken from *Why Pro-Life?* by Randy Alcorn:

> *Some Christian readers may think, "This book [Why Pro-Life?] isn't for us— it's unchurched people who are having abortions." In fact, 43 percent of women obtaining abortions identify themselves as Protestant, and 27 percent identify themselves as Catholic. So two-thirds of America's abortions are performed on women who identify themselves as born-again or evangelical*

*Christians. That's nearly a quarter-mil-
lion abortions each year in Bible-believ-
ing churches.*[3]

The abortion issue isn't about the church needing to speak to the world. It's about the church needing to speak to itself first, and then to the world. [2]

Those within church leadership must get their heads out of the proverbial sand and ask themselves why so many church-going women are having abortions? But more importantly, where are they failing to meet the needs of women in their churches that these women would even consider having an abortion? Abortion and the damage it does to the baby, mother, father and family should be openly discussed among the youth in churches BEFORE they are in the position to consider having one. Teaching abstinence is great, but for those who indulge in pre-marital sexual activity, and studies show that 90% will, abortion would rarely be considered an option if, starting at an early age, the teaching within our churches had built a Pro-life, Pro-justice mindset into the DNA of their youth.

Most churches have neglected the needs of their women and allowed injustice to prevail within their organizations for two generations. We will lose another generation if things don't change. Women and men in the church need to feel safe in telling their stories to the youth within their church, stories of how abortion has affected their lives and the pain and shame they have had to endure with the taking of the life of their child. **Silence on the injustice of abortion by church leadership and those affected by it only serves to perpetuate it.**

Most churches have a Men's Ministry and a Women's Ministry. The larger the church, the more likely they will have some sort of "Recovery Ministry" within their respective Men's or Women's Ministry. These Recovery Ministries are intended to help men or women through addictions or behavioral problems including: overeating, alcoholism, drug addictions, sexual addictions, pornography, gambling, anger and so forth.

Those leading these ministries need to be aware of a common denominator that has just recently come to light. If we peel back all of the layers and examine the root cause of many problems experienced by those in the church, we will be surprised to discover how many individuals, especially women, experience addictions or harmful behavioral issues as a result of a past abortion that has never been properly dealt with.

Abortion needs to be addressed within the church today, not only for the protection of our youth, but to rescue those that are desperate for help and healing. If a full third of our parishioners have participated in an abortion, then the potential impact is staggering!

As it relates to the Underground Railroad and properly serving the needs of women, here are a few things that those within the leadership of a church or religious organization may want to consider:

1. People who attend church are just as imperfect as everyone else; we all need forgiveness because we all have a past to deal with. One out of three men and women between the ages of twenty and sixty WITHIN YOUR CHURCH or organization has been involved in the unjust killing of their own child. Don't believe it? Start asking the people around you that know they can trust you. They're on your staff, your boards and on your stage/platform. They are your volunteers, and maybe you yourself have been involved with an abortion and have never told a soul. It's there. These people need to find healing and tell their stories.

2. Don't shoot your wounded….Make your church or organization a safe place. Everyone has a past and everyone has struggles; create a culture where people can be "real" and can be loved through whatever it is they need healing from or struggle with.

3. Encourage those within your church to volunteer and financially support the local Pregnancy Resource Center. Find out what is needed and make it your organization's mission to make certain they get it. What is most needed are people who will love women enough to do whatever is necessary to get them through and beyond an unplanned pregnancy. Like the slavery abolitionists who gave escaped slaves anything they needed to build a better life, abor-

tion abolitionists need to be willing to provide whatever help to women they are able and that is needed.

4. Lead well. People need leadership, but silence promotes injustice. Speak or permit others to speak to the injustice of abortion at every opportunity. Encourage those you lead to follow the **Change the Shame** "Battle Plan" and spread the word about **Change the Shame** to those they influence.

Together the churches and Pro-justice organizations can end the injustice of abortion within any community or city.

The abortion industry is the same as any business; a business will cease to operate when it is no longer profitable. With that basic economic principle in mind and the fact that 70% of the abortion industry's customers are coming from within the church, here is the formula to bring about an end to businesses providing abortions within any city:

To shut down the businesses providing abortions…. remove the profitability! To remove the profitability….remove the church from their customer base!

In other words, if the leadership within churches and religious organizations would make the commitment that they will do everything within their power to meet the needs of women facing an unplanned pregnancy and to make certain that the youth for whom they are responsible are taught the truth about abortion, businesses providing abortions will soon be gone from our communities.

All the resources an organization will ever need to expose the truth about abortion can be found at *ChangeTheShame.com*.

Endnotes

2   George Grant, *Third Time Around*, (Brentwood, TN: Wolgemuth & Hyatt, Publishers, Inc., 1991), p. 12.

3   Randy Alcorn, *Why Pro-Life? Caring for the Unborn and Their Mothers,* (Peabody, MA: Hendrickson Publishers, 2004), p. 17.

GROUP DISCUSSION— *The Underground Railroad*

Why do you think slave abolitionists would make such huge sacrifices and risk death and imprisonment for slaves, people they generally did not know and that could never repay them?

What characteristics do you think slave abolitionists of 150 years ago have in common with abortion abolitionists today?

The Author claims that once a woman is pregnant. Whether they decide to abort, adopt or raise the child, their life will never be the same. What do you think the Author means by this statement?

The quote by Randy Alcorn puts two-thirds of abortions as being performed on women who identify themselves as being born-again or evangelical Christians. What does this say about the church today?

The Author claims that abortion could be ended if those within the church were removed from the abortion industry's customer base. Do you agree? Why or why not?

If you attend a church, list 5 things that you think your church could start doing that would reduce the number of abortions in your community?

Read 2 Kings Chapter 20. King Hezekiah had done a foolish thing by showing visitors from Babylon all the treasures of his kingdom. In the admonishment delivered by Isaiah, Hezekiah was told that his descendants would be hauled off to Babylon and become eunuchs. Hezekiah considered this report to be good because it didn't affect him. What do you think Hezekiah's response to Isaiah's admonishment should have been?

When it comes to abortion, how might Hezekiah's response be viewed as being similar to the attitudes of some people today?

CHAPTER SEVEN
The Big Picture

"Speak up for those who cannot speak for themselves, for the rights of those who are destitute. Speak up and judge fairly; defend the rights of the poor and needy."

—King Solomon

Sometimes we are unable to see the forest for the trees. We expend so much effort in trying to save and nurture a single tree that we give no thought as to how we could possibly save the entire forest.

There is a "Micro" and a "Macro" side to this Second Civil War. The Micro side is what the Pro-life movement has been very proficient at for the past forty years. They have committed their efforts, marketing and resources to finding and helping local individual women who are facing an unplanned pregnancy. They seek local donors who are sympathetic with the Civil Right to Life of the unborn. Through the generous support of these donors, Pregnancy Resource Centers are able to provide services such as counseling, support systems, infant clothing and supplies, pregnancy tests and mobile medical clinics.

All these things are necessary because they provide for the physical and emotional needs of local women at their point of crisis. All these things have their place and purpose. The collective efforts of the millions of people involved at the local level make a huge impact, providing help to women and saving the lives of the unborn.

As great as the Pro-life Movement has been with the Micro side, we must realize that doing a stellar effort on the Micro side will never bring about an end to abortion within our nation. The abortion industry is not bothered by Pro-lifers finding and caring for the occasional tree as long as they continue to own the forest. While Micro is the work of caring for individual trees, Macro is the war that is needed to save the entire forest.

It would be highly unusual to find a Pregnancy Resource Center that has a plan for ending abortion within their city and even less likely that any national organization has developed a strategic plan for ending abortion in our nation. We have erroneously thought that the forest could be saved by simply finding and caring for more individual trees. It is like trying to end slavery by freeing more slaves.

Most books written on the topic of abortion are Micro focused, encouraging the reader to volunteer and financially support their local Pregnancy Resource Centers and national "Pro-life" organizations. Most books written about abortion are about finding and caring for more trees. Even though caring for more individual trees is important, this book is not about that; this book is primarily about the Macro; the Second Civil War is about saving the forest.

This book responds to the question, **"How do we END the injustice of abortion within the USA?"** This book is about Pro-justice and presenting the truth that abortion denies the Civil Liberties promised to all Americans in our Constitution. This book is meant to challenge those within the Pro-life Movement to realize, while their intentions are honorable, their current methods and strategies will never bring about the desired outcome— the end of abortion. This book is about bringing renewed hope and passion to those that have faithfully supported the Rights of the unborn but have grown weary and disheartened from the lack of any meaningful progress these past forty years.

Contrary to the opinions of many, abortion is not a political issue; it is a Civil Rights issue. It is the responsibility of our government to protect the rights of its people; this responsibility must be extended to citizens that are still developing within their mother's womb. But just like the slaves, these unborn citizens have no power, no voice and no vote. All the more reason our government needs to protect them. We must become their power, voice and vote.

Our Founding Fathers understood that governments don't make laws and governments don't make decisions, people do. And if the people who are entrusted with decision-making power ignore or fail to understand that it is the responsibility of the government to protect the Rights of its citizens, then it's time to remind them of their responsibility by replacing them with others who do.

History reveals that elected officials have passed laws contrary to the Civil Rights of individual citizens and history has also revealed that our system of checks and balances has at times failed to overturn these laws that infringe on these Rights. The Supreme Court decision in the abortion case of Roe v. Wade failed to nullify laws that trample the Rights of citizens in the same way that the Dred Scott Decision of 1857 and the Plessy v. Ferguson Decision of 1896 failed to do.

As American citizens we have the responsibility to elect leaders who have the integrity necessary to pass laws that protect the unborn and to change the makeup of the Supreme Court so that there are enough Supreme Court Justices who will stand for justice and overturn Roe v. Wade.

As was the case with other nations, it certainly would have been better for all involved if slave-owners had agreed to free their slaves and the U.S. Government had offered some form of compensation to these slave-owners in return. Prior to the Civil War many in the South enjoyed great wealth, leisure and society. A plan to compensate slave-owners in exchange for their slave's freedom certainly would have been less costly than the war. Hindsight is always 20/20, but the capital of men and wealth lost by the South during the Civil War has taken 150 years to recover and even so, much of the South remains impoverished today.

The losses suffered by the South during the Civil War should serve as a lesson to abortion proponents. It would be nice if we all could simply agree that abortion is an injustice and that it violates the Civil Rights of the unborn. How glorious it would be if the shame of abortion would just go away and no one had to endure any pain or suffer any loss. **THIS IS NOT GOING TO HAPPEN!!** In the early 1800s our political leaders negotiated compromise after compromise to keep the nation from blowing apart over the issue of slavery. These compromises worked for a while, but eventually the pressure from the opposing forces was too great and as a result our nation was almost destroyed. The longer we postpone doing the right thing by recognizing the Civil Rights of the unborn the more painful the inevitable move to justice will be. In other words, there is no doubt: abortion will eventually end; but the longer those advocating abortion hold out the more painful their capitulation will be.

As things stand today, there are no silver bullets, no magic wands, no last minute compromises and no miraculous happy endings. Just as the slave-owners had to endure tremendous emotional and financial pain before submitting to what was right, so will those extremists in the Pro-abortion camp. I hope that I'm wrong.

The question remains: Are there enough people who care about justice for the unborn and who are willing to take the actions necessary to inflict the level of pain required to move the Pro-abortion camp to capitulation? Can a large enough Pro-justice army be united to cause fear of financial and political ruin for those who advocate or are "neutral" on abortion? Are there enough people to get this done TODAY or must we wait another forty years and allow another fifty-five million of our fellow citizens to be destroyed before we find another generation that has the courage to go to war?

Freeing individual slaves one at a time was heroic and rewarding to those actively participating, but no matter how many slaves the Underground Railroad freed it was never enough to bring about an end to slavery. Helping individual women must continue and will always be important, but no matter how many babies are saved it will never be enough to end abortion.

If you haven't figured it out by now, there is a great deal of work to be done. Individuals and organizations must continue to serve young women at every opportunity (Micro). But every Pro-life or Pro-justice individual and organization must constantly be asking the bigger (Macro) question, "What must we do to end abortion in our community and nation?"

It will only be through the collective and collaborative efforts of millions of Americans with singularity of purpose that the injustice of abortion will end.

GROUP DISCUSSION— *The Big Picture*

When it comes to the abortion battle, describe in your own words the difference between the Micro and the Macro?

The Author claims that when it comes to ending abortion within our nation, the Pro-Life Movement has made little meaningful progress the past forty years. Would you agree or disagree? Why?

Do you vote on a regular basis?

If so, what criteria do you use in selecting which candidates you vote for?

Have you read anything in this book that might change or reinforce your voting responsibility or the criteria you use to select which candidates you vote for? If so, how?

Read James 1:19-27. This short passage delivers some very powerful instruction for followers of Christ and concludes that Religion accepted by God is to "look after orphans and widows in their distress and to keep oneself from being polluted by the world". Knowing God's heart regarding orphans and widows, what do you think would be God's heart regarding the protection of the unborn?

The Author claims that abortion will eventually end and that future generations will look at our generation in disbelief that so many could advocate the killing of children just as we look in disbelief at former generations' slave ownership and rampant racial discrimination. What are your thoughts?

CHAPTER EIGHT

The Battle Plan

"The only thing necessary for the triumph of evil is for good men to do nothing."

—Edmund Burke

A s previously stated, the United States is about to embark on its Second Civil War. This next Civil War will be fought to abolish the injustice of abortion, but this Civil War will NOT be fought on battlefields or the streets of our cities. Because the abortion industry is backed by powerful and wealthy individuals, these individuals must feel intense financial pain and be stripped of their political power. For this to happen, the war to abolish abortion will be fought in the marketplace, in the polls and in the hearts and minds of the American people.

Slavery Abolitionists were threatened and ridiculed. They made great sacrifices of their wealth, reputation and time for the freedom of people they would probably never know. Serious Abortion Abolitionists should be prepared to experience the same treatment and sacrifice for the Civil Rights of the unborn. These hardships can be considered a badge of honor, because someday people will look back and view those who endured these hardships as heroes of their time. Future generations will view them with the same reverence that we now view those who sacrificed so much to end slavery and racial discrimination.

How quickly abortion is abolished is really up to each of us and our willingness to do the things necessary to bring it to an end. There are those who are fully committed to abolishing this injustice, but just as it was with slavery, many will remain apathetic. We must each ask ourselves the questions, **"How do we END the injustice of abortion within the USA?"** and **"AM I willing to do my part to end it?"**

In Chapter Three you were presented the opportunity to rate yourself on this scale:

On a scale of 1-10 how would you rate your position on abortion?

1 ___ 2 ___ 3 ___ 4 ___ 5 ___ 6 ___ 7 ___ 8 ___ 9 ___ 10
Strongly Pro-abortion   Neutral   Strongly Pro-justice

If you honestly cannot rate yourself as a "10" you might as well stop reading and put this book away. When you reach the point where you are sickened with the killing of the unborn as much as you are sickened by the slaughter of school children huddled in the corner of their classrooms, pick up this book again, enlist in the war and put action to your outrage.

THERE IS NO NEUTRALITY! Anyone who is not Pro-justice is Anti-justice. One may even convince themselves that "Pro-choice" is a form of neutrality. Wrong! Being "Pro-choice" is the same as being "Pro-slavery"; it keeps the power in the hands of those who violate the rights of another. Apathy and neutrality by the majority of Americans prolonged slavery for ninety years. In the same way, the abortion industry knows that as long as they can convince the American people that a neutral or Pro-choice position is acceptable, injustice will continue to be victorious.

It is time for Pro-justice Americans to go on the offensive and put the abortion industry on the defensive. No surprises, no need for war rooms and no need to keep the battle plan a secret. The economic and political power of Pro-justice Americans will be leveraged in such a way that Pro-justice businesses and political leaders are greatly rewarded. They will be rewarded and entrusted with dollars and votes so that they may use their new-found wealth and power to effect the changes needed. If they violate this trust, others will be found to replace them. Lip-service won't cut it; lead, or get out of the way.

Being "Pro-life" is good. But being "Pro-life only means that you have taken a position. Change the Shame is so much more; **Change the Shame is a CALL TO ACTION.** A call to action for those who recognize that abortion not only is a shameful injustice that deprives fellow citizens of their Civil Rights, but that abortion is harmful to the men and women having them, harmful to their families, and harmful to our entire nation.

Change the Shame has begun the creation of a nation-wide network of millions of people that are committed to making the changes needed to protect the unborn. There is no doubt that new strategies will emerge as different tactics prove to be more or less effective, but these ideas and strategies are kept up-to-date on *ChangeTheShame.com*. The following list is merely a starting point.

Start by examining yourself. Do you harbor hatred or animosity toward men or women who have believed the deception of the abortion industry and have been involved in an abortion themselves? Don't! It accomplishes nothing.

Are your words and statements about abortion Life-giving or Life-sucking? In other words, when you have a conversation about abortion, do those who hold a different opinion feel they've been in an intelligent conversation or a heated argument? Our battle is not against those who have been wounded, but rather against those that are inflicting the wounds; those who have become wealthy through deceptively promoting abortion as a good thing for women and society.

Refrain from arguing with, shouting at, embarrassing, using negative posters, using violence or condemning anyone who may disagree with you or has experienced an abortion in the past. We must recognize both our own imperfections and our responsibility to expose the truth and offer forgiveness and healing to the wounded.

Remove any bumper sticker that says anything similar to, "Abortion is Murder" and replace it with a bumper sticker that merely says, "Change the Shame." Get one for each vehicle at *ChangeTheShame.com*. Remember, we're not denying that abortion is murder. We're simply abandoning a method that has failed to be effective.

Get a copy of the Change the Shame Pledge and sign it. You can obtain a copy in the back of this book or at *ChangeTheShame.com*. Feel free to copy The Pledge and use it as often as you like, but do not change The Pledge in any way.

Go to Facebook and "Like" the Change the Shame page. Also go to the page of your nearest Pregnancy Resource Center and "Like" their page as well. By "Liking" these pages you will have access to all sorts of events and activities that are happening both locally and nationally. Facebook users will receive fresh and relevant information as to how the battle is progressing and the tactics used in each victory. Facebook and other social media sites will not only keep the fight for justice in the forefronts of our minds, but they will also be the means of communicating important information to the masses of troops. Social media will take you from being a casual observer to an active participant.

Change the Shame Facebook
Page can be found at:
*https://www.facebook.com/
pages/Change-the-Shame/
450048381713502?ref=hl*

Get the free mobile app at
http://gettag.mobi

Scan the QR code above with
your mobile device to go directly
to the Facebook page.

**If you attend a church get a copy of this book into
the hands of your church leadership and insist they
read it.** Church leadership needs to understand that
70% of those having abortion claim to be Christians
(Catholic or Protestant) and that the culture within
many Churches, though unintentional, actually encourages abortion rather than discouraging it. *Change
the Shame* should become part of your church mission, and the injustice of abortion openly talked about
with young people BEFORE they find themselves in
an unplanned pregnancy.

Young people need to be firmly Pro-justice before
they are ever in a situation where they need to make
a "choice." Trying to convince women that abortion
is not the best "choice" at the time of their crisis is
too late. Young men and women need to be taught the
value of justice for all, including the unborn, BEFORE
they are in the position of having to consider abortion
as an option.

Maybe your children and the youth in your church
will never have sex before they are married and will

never face the choice of an abortion. But even if they never experience this "choice", they know others who will. Equip them with tools so that they will be able to help those who need it. Instill Pro-justice messaging into the lives of your youth so that Pro-justice is part of their DNA long before their dating years.

Join the Underground Railroad. Volunteer in and financially support the local efforts to aid young men and women who need help with an adoption or in raising their child. What this means will vary from city to city and community to community. Your local Pregnancy Resource Center should have an Underground Railroad Coordinator to build the services needed in your community. If they don't have a coordinator then help them see the need of having one and offer your assistance in raising the necessary funding to get your local Underground Railroad started.

Patronize *Change the Shame* businesses. How cool would it be to see a *Change the Shame* decal on the front door of your favorite businesses? What about the *Change the Shame* logo on the websites where you shop online? What if businesses started adding the statement, "*Change the Shame*" at the end of every TV or radio advertisement? What if there were a search engine that identified all *Change the Shame* endorsed businesses? What if there were a website that listed only *Change the Shame* endorsed businesses in any given city or geographical area?

What if millions of Americans drew a line in the sand and said we will not spend one more dime on groceries, insurance, banking services, pharmaceuticals, auto repair, restaurants, medical care or even a cup of coffee at any business that is not *Change the Shame* endorsed? What if millions of American business owners not only became *Change the Shame* endorsed, but only made purchases for their business from other *Change the Shame* endorsed businesses?

Imagine a national insurance company coming out with an announcement that they have just been endorsed by *Change the Shame*. And then the very next day millions of Americans cancel their home and auto insurance policies only to transfer their insurance policies to the newly endorsed *Change the Shame* company? Wouldn't this get the attention of the national media and encourage other businesses to follow suit? Just as the news of battles kept the Civil War and the fight against slavery forefront in the minds of the American people, so will these great financial and political battles keep the fight against abortion prominent in our thoughts.

Imagine what can be accomplished if millions of Americans channel their economic and political power in a united effort! But everyone who is sickened and saddened by the injustice of abortion must be willing to do their part; it takes a lot of rain drops to create a raging flood.

Become an Officer or Foot Soldier in the War. The roles of Officers and Foot Soldiers will develop and evolve over time but it is certain that leaders and teams will be needed in every town and city across this country. We will need teams to help identify and recruit businesses to become Change the Shame endorsed. Speakers must rise up and become skilled to make Change the Shame presentations in schools, churches, businesses and other organizations. Just as with any war, funds will be needed to continue the fight. We must create distributors and distribution channels to sell Change the Shame apparel, books, bumper stickers and other merchandise to raise the needed funds. Visit *ChangeTheShame.com* to see what enlistment opportunities are available in your area.

Read, Learn and Become Articulate. Review the arguments that were used to defend slavery; they are the same arguments used to defend abortion. By showing the parallels between the slavery arguments and the abortion arguments, people will see how intellectually dishonest those arguments are. At *ChangeTheShame. com* is a "resources" tab where you'll find resources including books, websites, videos and articles. These resources will empower you to be able to speak the truth about the injustice of abortion, an injustice no different than slavery or racial discrimination.

Be an active listener so that when an opportunity or "teachable moment" presents itself, you are fully capable of planting the seed of justice with those you know.

Get a Copy of this Book into the Hands of Every Business Owner You Know and Insist They Read IT. Only do this with business owners that you currently support; if you're not supporting their business your opinion means nothing. Let them know that from

this day forward you will be supporting businesses endorsed by *Change the Shame.* If a business has
Pro-justice ownership that you think should be endorsed by Change the Shame, have the owner visit
ChangetheShame.com to get them started in the en-
dorsement process.

Change the Shame does not endorse businesses to
make business owners or stockholders wealthy.
Change the Shame endorses businesses so that these
business owners and stockholders will have the financial resources needed to make sizable contributions
to their local Pregnancy Resource Centers as they develop their local Underground Railroad. Individuals
only have so much money they can donate to their
local Pregnancy Resource Centers. But if a small percentage of all the various places we Americans spend
money is being channeled back into Pro-justice efforts, the funding provided to these organizations
would be phenomenal.

For example, you may not have an extra $100 or $200
per month to contribute to organizations defending the rights of the unborn. But consider if just one
percent of the $3000 per month you're spending on
groceries, healthcare, housing, insurance, fuel and so
forth were channeled back into these organizations.
Now multiply that figure by hundreds or thousands
of families within your community. In this way, these
organizations would have all the resources necessary
to win the war.

Only Support and Vote for Pro-justice Political Candidates. Put a copy of this book into the hands of everyone you know holding or running for political office and let them know that if they aren't Pro-justice they'd better become Pro-justice or find other employment. Members of the media have brutalized Pro-life candidates in recent elections. These candidates need to rebrand themselves as being Pro-justice (rather than Pro-life) and become articulate on the similarities between abortion, slavery and racial discrimination.

Draw another line in the sand; make the commitment that you will never again vote for any political candidate who does not strongly oppose abortion. Don't buy into the lie that this or that candidate is "the lesser of two evils." If both or all candidates support abortion then vote for none of them. When you find an uncompromising, Pro-justice political candidate, get behind them with all of the support you can offer and afford.

Change the Shame will only endorse political candidates who have signed the *Change the Shame Pledge* and can demonstrate a history of being sympathetic with the Civil Rights of the unborn. Check out *ChangeTheShame.com* for candidates endorsed in your area.

Turn Off the Television and Radio. Understand that much of the media is controlled by individuals sympathetic with the abortion industry. As *Change the Shame* gains momentum, making positive strides in changing the hearts and minds of the American people, these puppet media groups will be ruthless in their coverage of *Change the Shame*. Expect it, plan on it but don't be fooled by it. Only time will tell what measures will be taken to attempt to shut down and shut up *Change the Shame*. All the more reason to take your patronage to businesses that are *Change the Shame* endorsed.

If your business becomes *Change the Shame* endorsed, then refuse to advertise or promote your business in any media or advertising venue that is not *Change the Shame* endorsed. Imagine a TV station that is controlled by a Pro-abortion manager that elects to run a "news" story trashing a Pro-justice organization. Imagine the day following this news story that thirty business owners call the station to cancel their advertising campaigns. Do you think this station manager might rethink things the next time he is tempted to run another "news" story intended to brainwash the uninformed? These are the types of battles we need to have and win.

Become Active in Local School Boards. Local School Boards welcome your involvement and participation. They remain one of the few political entities where your opinions can directly influence its direction. This book highlights valuable historical lessons regarding the actions, both right and wrong, taken by our nation's leaders on the issues of slavery, women's suffrage and civil rights. Knowing and understanding history is the first step to prevent making the same mistakes with abortion that we made with slavery.

There are hundreds of thousands of teachers and school administrators who oppose the injustice conferred upon the unborn through abortion. Use your influence and connections to have this book become part of the history and social studies curriculum within your local Middle Schools and High Schools by offering a copy to teachers and school administrators you know well.

Adopt. Just as the abolition of slavery created other social challenges, so the abolition of abortion will bring its own set of social challenges. We must be mindful that there are many reasons why women feel that abortion is their only choice. These reasons will continue long after abortion has ended. For instance, many women cannot or should not be raising a child. But the mother's inability to raise a child should not be a death sentence for the child. Of the women who understand this, many will make the heroic choice of placing their child in the hands of others more capable of giving their child a chance at a life of happiness and fulfillment. You have an endless capacity for love; **consider adopting a child**.

If you feel you are beyond the age of raising more children, consider becoming Godparents. Maybe you have grown children or know of a younger family who is capable and desirous of adopting a child but they lack the financial means to do so. Make arrangements so that they take the parenting responsibility while you shoulder some or much of the financial responsibility.

Memorialized in the movie, ***Schindler's List***, Oskar Schindler left a legacy using his fortune to save hundreds of Jews from Hitler's cruel death camps. Thousands of slavery abolitionists made great financial sacrifice for people they would never know and who could never repay. Abortion abolitionists must have the same selfless, sacrificial attitude when it comes to aiding the unborn. Your actions may never be memorialized in a movie, but the legacy you'll leave through the lives you save will have eternal impact.

Finally, get a Copy of this Book into the Hands of Ten People You Know Well. Don't just buy several copies and mail them; make a list of ten people with whom you are well connected. Call, text or email them to let them know you're sending them a book and ask them to read it as a personal favor to you. After they have read this book, meet with them to get their feedback and to determine if they have the same commitment to abolishing abortion as you. Then support and encourage them as they follow through and act on the list of action items that you have acted upon. Here is a list to help you identify the ten people you should contact:

Employer _____

Teacher _____

Elected Official or Representative _____

_____

Business Owner _____

Business Owner_____

Pastor or Ministry Leader _____

_____

Person in Media _____

Family Member_____

Close Friend _____

Close Friend _____

It would be very easy to just finish this chapter, turn the page and not take a single action from the items you just read. By ourselves, change will never happen; it is only through the collective efforts by all of us that change will occur. I challenge you: **Do not turn this page until you have at least started.** "Like" the *Change the Shame* Facebook page. Write down ten names of people you'd like to get a copy of this book to. Go to *ChangeTheShame.com* and order those ten books. Step out and begin Changing the Shame! Taking the first step is the hardest part of any journey; you'll be glad you did.

GROUP DISCUSSION— *The Battle Plan*

After going through this book, on the scale of 1-10, how did you rate your position on abortion this time?

Read Mark 9:33-41. As Christ-followers we do what we know to be right, not because of wanting to leave a legacy, be praised by others or for some other earthly reward, but we do what we believe to be right because we have within us the heart of God. It is having within us the heart of God that alone compels us to take action when we see an injustice or a need. To quote Edmund Burke, "The only thing necessary for the triumph of evil is for good men to do nothing." Share any thoughts you might have regarding the previous statement, including how you think God might view situations where good men see evil and do nothing?

According to the Author, neutrality on abortion is the same as being Pro-abortion. What does this mean to you?

Most people who read this book will put it on the shelf when finished and do nothing to take part in the battle to end abortion. How would you describe your willingness to take part in the battle to protect the Right to Life of the unborn?

Many think that a charismatic leader like Martin Luther King Jr. will come along to lead us through the abortion battle and on to victory. The Author maintains that the end of abortion will only happen if millions of Pro-justice people all do their part. Do you believe that you have the ability and the responsibility to protect the Civil Rights of the unborn?

If so, of the items listed in "The Battle Plan" what specific items will you do?

Who will you ask to hold you accountable to do your part?

Have you prayerfully considered who you should give a copy of this book to? ....

Who? ....

....

....

....

....

(Note: *Keep in mind, people will not generally go out and buy a book on abortion or even read one if given to them. You will notice that abortion is not mentioned anywhere on the cover and the word is not mentioned until well into the book. The intent is not to be deceptive but rather to allow the truth to penetrate those who would otherwise have a closed or apathetic mind. When you give out copies of this book tell people that the book is an interesting twist on Civil Rights, ask them to read it as a favor to you and then have a follow-up visit to get their feedback.*)

What other ideas do you have that could help bring abortion to an end within your community? ....

....

....

....

....

....

CHAPTER NINE
Finding Our Way

"I've noticed that everyone who is for abortion has already been born."

—Ronald Reagan

A group of people are out for a hike in the mountains of Colorado. The person at the head of the group is confidently leading the way while the rest of the group blindly follows, chatting with each other without paying much attention to where they are going. The trail started off as well traveled, but after the trail had forked a few times it became less and less perceivable.

The members of the party start to privately wonder if anyone is really certain about where they are going, and after a while someone speaks out to question the leader. The leader has been uncertain about where he was going for some time but just continued to lead in hopes he would figure things out before anyone else caught on. The group finally comes to the realization that they are lost.

In these types of situations there are normally two responses. The first and most common response is for followers to start blaming others for where they are. "What were you thinking?" "Why didn't you turn right?" "You should have done this or that!" "It's all your fault!" "I really didn't want to go on a hike to begin with!" Their focus is on the **cause** of the problem rather than **solving** the problem.

The second, less common response is from those with true leadership ability. These individuals understand that, for the moment, how the group arrived at being lost is irrelevant and that reaching a consensus on who is to blame or what went wrong will not improve the situation. Their attitude is simply, "We are lost, that's the situation, now let's deal with it." These individuals focus all of their mental and physical energy on one simple thing: "What must be done to find our way home?"

When it comes to abortion, *our nation is lost.* Somewhere along the way we have strayed away from the path of justice and respect for human life. We have leadership hoping that no one notices and that the masses will continue to blindly follow. As with the hiking group that started noticing that things just didn't look right, we too are starting to notice little things. And when things appear amiss, like some demented individual entering an elementary school and slaughtering innocent children, many will play the blame game. "Not enough gun control!" "Video games are too violent!" "School security is the problem!" We've heard them all.

The truth is: WE ARE LOST. We have created a society that doesn't value human life and blaming other things will not change that fact. We are where we are…. "We are lost, that's the situation, now let's deal with it"…. Now is the time for true leadership to step forward and help us find our way back to where we should be.

The abolition of slavery and the Civil Rights Movement provided course corrections for our nation and the abolition of abortion will do the same, but leaders are needed. Leaders like the dozens of individuals and organizations listed in George Grant's book, *Third Time Around.* But a few dozen is just the beginning; millions more are needed.

Examples of this leadership, people with boots on the ground today, can be found all over the internet. *3801Lancaster.com* is a documentary website dedicated to exposing the case of Philadelphia abortionist, Kermit Gosnell. If you still don't believe this nation is lost, watch their video; the QR code to the right will link you to it.

Get the free mobile app at
http://gettag.mobi

There is a scene in this video where the leaders of the Black Pro-Life Coalition are gathered outside the Women's Medical Society Abortion Clinic at 3801 Lancaster in Philadelphia, the clinic of the infamous abortionist Kermit Gosnell. In this video an unidentified black woman makes this statement:

> *"Abortion is the number one killer of African Americans; killing more black people than all other deaths combined.... I think there are many of us who have forgotten what the 'dream' was all about. Civil Rights are still being violated. Even today, how many black people continue to look the other way while black babies are being slaughtered by abortionists? How can we continue to smile, slapping each other on the back, proud of our accomplishments when abortion facilities are purposefully placed in inner city and minority neighborhoods to crush the bodies of innocent black children? Make no mistake; abortion is a Civil Rights issue!"*

In this same video an unidentified black man, who appears to be another member of the same Black Pro-life Coalition, makes this profound statement:

> *"Everything that was ever gained in the Civil Rights Movement means nothing to a dead black child."*

People like this man and woman are the heroes and leaders that we need today. If anyone in this country ought to know about injustice, it is Black Americans. The people in this 3801 Lancaster video understand the battle, but why do the majority of other Black Americans "look the other way" while their race is being targeted for "slaughter"? Have most Black Americans traded their slavery to a plantation owner for slavery to a political mind-set that keeps them in chains just as much as slavery did? Black Americans, where are you? We need you like never before; the unborn beg you to speak up, stop the injustice and come to their defense.

We also need millions of men and women who are willing to step forward and share their stories. Stories such as the ones told in Rob Fischer's book, *13 Jars*. Women are being lied to. Those who have experienced abortions are needed to let others know the truth: the physical and emotional pain of ending the life of their child greatly exceeds the temporary pain of handing their child over to be raised by another. Or the truth that being a parent isn't the end of your world; raising a child can be a wonderful thing.

Just as photos and stories of slavery propelled slavery abolitionists into action so will the personal stories of regretted abortions encourage many to enlist in the battle against it. Learn how you can find healing from your past abortion or how your story can help others by visiting the Abortion Anonymous website, *AbAnon.org.*

During a war people sometimes change sides. The person changing sides is identified in both a positive term and a negative term: *defector* or *traitor*. The term used for the same individual depends on which side you are on; *defector* if you're on the new side and *traitor* if on the former. Being labeled a *defector* is good; being labeled a *traitor* is not. As the abortion Civil War unfolds and as more and more people realize the truth we will see and hear more stories from these defectors.

One such defector and hero is former abortionist Dr. Anthony Levatino. There is quite a bit of information about Dr. Levatino on the internet but **Dr. Levatino's Story** and **HR 3803** are two must-watch videos for anyone who considers themself "Pro-life", "Pro-justice", "Pro-Civil Rights" or "Pro-Human Rights." However, anyone who is "Pro-choice" and is determined to remain that way regardless of the facts or arguments should not view these videos; they WILL change your mind.

Here are a few of the statements made by Dr. Levatino:

> *"I've never actually counted. I'm glad I can't say that I'm responsible for 50,000 plus abortions, but I know I've done hundreds of the procedures. That's direct, hands-on involvement, with the forceps in your hand, reaching into somebody's uterus and tearing out a baby."*

"Why do doctors do abortions? There are many reasons. It's profitable, there's a lot of money in it! But there's philosophical things that come first. As I'm fond of telling people, if you are Pro-choice and you happen to be a gynecologist, then it's up to you to take the instruments in hand and actively perform an abortion. It's the most natural association in the world. Along the way you find out you make a lot of money doing abortions. In my practice we were averaging between $250 and $500 for an abortion, and it was cash."

"There are other reasons; they're perhaps no less important. I've heard many times from other obstetricians: Well, I'm not really pro-abortion, I'm pro-woman. How many times have you heard that one? The women's groups in this country, they're not alone, but they've done a very good job selling that bill of goods to the population. That somehow destroying a life is pro-woman. But a lot of obstetricians use that justification to themselves, and I can tell you, a lot of them believe it. I used to. It's not hard to be convinced of it."

"When the abortionist finishes a suction D & C, he has to open a little suc-

tion bag and he has to literally reassemble the child. He has to do that because he wants to make sure he didn't leave anything behind."

"I had complications, just like everybody else. I have perforated uteruses. I have had all kinds of problems — bleeding, infection — Lord knows how many of those women are sterile now."

"As a doctor, you know that these are children; you know that these are human beings with arms and legs and heads and they move around and they are very active. But you get reminded — every time you put that scanner down on somebody's uterus — you are reminded. Because you see the children in there — hearts beating, arms flinging."

"After a few months of that I started to realize — this is somebody's child. I lost my child, someone who was very precious to us. And now I am taking somebody's child and I am tearing him right out of their womb. I am killing somebody's child."

"That is what it took to get me to change. My own sense of self-esteem went down the tubes. I began to feel like a paid assassin. That's exactly what I was. It got

to the point where it just wasn't worth it to me anymore. It was costing me too much personally. All the money in the world wouldn't have made a difference."

Please take a few minutes and view Dr. Levatino's story at: *http://www.youtube.com/ watch?v=F2pqZaQWlec*

Get the free mobile app at
http://gettag.mobi

Scanning this QR Code with your mobile device will take you there as well.

Another moving video of Dr. Levatino is the video of him providing testimony on HR 3803, the "District of Columbia Pain-Capable Child Protection Act." I'm confident that if this testimony video was viewed by every twelve-year old they would determine right then and there that, if they ever found themselves facing an unplanned pregnancy, abortion would never be the "choice" for their unborn child.

Please take the time to view Dr. Levatino's testimony at: *http://www.youtube.com/watch?v=t--MhKiaD7c*

Scanning this QR Code with your mobile device will take you there as well.

Get the free mobile app at
http://gettag.mobi

Slave owners knew that ending slavery would forever change the economic model on which they relied, so they were committed in their attempt to preserve slavery until the bitter end. For the vast majority of wealthy individuals in the South, the Civil War and the end of slavery brought financial ruin. Most abortionists are in the very same position; ending abortion will be their financial ruin.

What if there are hundreds of abortionists who are truly haunted by what they do but can't see any way out? What if these abortionists were offered grace, mercy and assistance by the Pro-justice community? What if local Pregnancy Resource Centers could raise enough funds to provide financial support to defecting abortionists while they sought an alternative means of supporting themselves? What if we extended the offer of help to see who might respond? Imagine dozens of other former abortionists, just like Dr. Levatino, out telling their stories in public hearings, in schools, in churches and to civic organizations throughout our nation.

What If…………?

We just might find our way home!

GROUP DISCUSSION— *Finding Our Way*

Did you watch the three videos introduced in this chapter? If not, go back and watch them. If this book hasn't convinced you that we have the responsibility to be the voice for the unborn surely these videos will.

What stood out the most as you were watching the 3801 Lancaster video?

In your opinion, how can it be that "black people continue to look the other way while black babies are being slaughtered by abortionists" and support political candidates and elected officials that openly advocate the practice?

What stood out the most as you were watching the Dr. Levatino videos?

The Author maintains that there are probably hundreds of abortionists who are haunted by what they do just as Dr. Levatino was. What do you think needs to happen for dozens of other abortionists to become defectors?

Read James 2:14-26. How does this passage relate to what we've learned about the injustice of abortion and our role to bring it to an end?

Conclusion

Eugenics is a philosophy that advocates the practice of promoting higher reproduction of more desirable people and traits and reduced reproduction of less desirable people and traits. Adolf Hitler, the leader of Germany during WWII, and Margaret Sanger, the founder of Planned Parenthood, are two of the most well-known names associated with Eugenics. Both of these individuals can be credited with the destruction of millions of lives at the hands of the organizations they created.

Eugenics is an acceptable and common practice when breeding horses, cattle or dogs, but when it comes to human beings, it is simply wrong. No human being should have the power to determine which physical characteristics or human traits are desirable and which are not, and thus control who may have children and who may not. The other problem with Eugenics in human breeding is that humans are going to breed and have offspring whether or not the people in power like their physical traits. The only way to keep them from breeding is to kill them.

Imagine that a prenatal test is developed to determine whether an unborn child will grow up to be bald. At the same time imagine that the people in control of some government determine that being bald is an undesirable trait and bald men and women should not be permitted to have children. Everyone who is bald, as well as their offspring, is then ordered to undergo a sterilization procedure that would prevent the spreading of the bald gene, and any woman who is pregnant must have the prenatal test performed and the baby terminated if it is found to have this undesirable bald gene.

The above illustration may seem absurd, but the truth is that this is exactly what Hitler and Sanger intended to do, but their targets were Jews and Blacks rather than the bald. Now think of your own undesirable characteristics; replace bald with too short, too fat, too thin, too weak, not attractive enough, not intelligent enough and so on.

What if a test was developed to determine who had the greatest chance of becoming Gay or having a low IQ and these tests were done early in a pregnancy? If the mother didn't like the results of the Gay or IQ test she could then decide to abort the child. Still think this is absurd? The truth is that the elimination of the homosexual population was one of the targets of eugenics in the early 20th Century. It may not be Gay or IQ testing today, but this is exactly what we have happening in our nation with the developmentally disabled.

Amniocentesis is a test commonly performed on women during their pregnancy to diagnose chromosomal or other fetal abnormalities such as Down Syndrome. If the results of the test indicate that the child has a high likelihood of having Down Syndrome the mother is often encouraged to terminate the pregnancy. This is a blatant violation of Human Rights; terminating a life solely because of a characteristic thought by someone to be undesirable.

Spend a chunk of your life raising a child with Down Syndrome and you'll be convinced that these are the most precious human beings ever to walk this planet; what they lack in ability they make up in the love they freely give. If we apathetically stand by and do nothing while Eugenics is being practiced on those with Down Syndrome today, what class of citizen will be next tomorrow?

You have just finished reading some very compelling arguments that abortion is a great injustice. As with slavery, denying women the right to vote, and racial discrimination, so the injustice of abortion must end. It took a Civil War to end slavery. It will take a Second Civil War to end abortion. This Second Civil War will not be fought with guns or violence, but will be fought with dollars and votes.

Some women will claim that they have no regret in having had an abortion and that they would do it again under similar circumstances. Similarly, if slavery were still permitted today there are still those who would love to own a few.

The final chapter of *Change the Shame* has yet to be written and you can influence the outcome. As a nation, we have the blood of fifty-five million babies on our hands and this number grows daily. What happens from this point is up to you. If you haven't enlisted already, please go back to **The Battle Plan** (Chapter 8) to determine what you can do to help us **Change the Shame**.

"The ones who are crazy enough to think that they can change the world, are the ones who do."

—Steve Jobs—

ChangeTheShame.com

GROUP DISCUSSION— *Conclusion*

In this conclusion the Author introduces the philosophy of Eugenics. In what ways could Eugenics benefit society?

In what ways is Eugenics harmful to society?

Take a moment to really examine your own heart; in your opinion, is there any class of people where amniocentesis should be used for targeting the unborn for elimination?

Think about where you spend your money and the businesses you support. What businesses do you support that DO NOT share your values?

What businesses do you support that you know for certain share your values?

Are there changes that need to be made?

Read Luke 10:25-37. In this story of the Good Samaritan there are three people who come across the Jewish traveler who had been beaten, robbed and left to die. If you were in a situation similar to this, would your response be similar to the Priest and Levite or would your response be similar to that of the Samaritan? (Why?)

Now think of the same story but replace the Jewish Traveler with the Unborn Child. Is your answer to the previous question consistent with the reality of the world we're living in today? In other words, Unborn Children are the Jewish Travelers of today; is your response the same as the Priest and Levite or is your response similar to the Samaritan's?

In what ways has this book challenged your thinking about abortion?

▶ Have you ever had an abortion or participated in an abortion?

▶ If so, have you ever participated in a Post-Abortive Recovery Class?

▶ If you have been involved in an abortion and never participated in a Post-Abortive Recovery, please visit *AbAnon.Org* or contact your local Pregnancy Resource Center.

Change the Shame Pledge

1. I recognize that abortion is a great INJUSTICE to the unborn and it is my responsibility to defend their Unalienable Rights to LIFE, LIBERTY and the pursuit of HAPPINESS.

2. I will stand for the rights of the unborn: never to participate in or encourage another to participate in an abortion.

3. I will stand in grace: never to condemn or judge anyone who has participated in an abortion

4. I will stand in peace: only opposing abortion through NON-VIOLENT means.

5. I will exercise my power to vote: giving my vote only to political candidates who openly support the abolishment of abortion.

6. I will exercise my economic power: to the extent possible, I will only patronize **Change the Shame** endorsed businesses that openly support the abolishment of abortion.

7. I will volunteer and give: I will physically and financially support, to the best of my ability, organizations whose mission is to protect the life and rights of the unborn.

8. I will educate myself: I will endeavor to understand the heartache of abortion and will seek to skillfully and respectfully respond to the intellectually dishonest arguments defending it.

9. I will be resolute: I will be unashamed of my stance for justice for the unborn. Even if ridiculed, I will verbally and visually support the abolishment of abortion at each opportunity.

Signed this _____ day of _____, 20___.

_____
Signature

Resources

Dozens if not hundreds of books, videos, personal interviews and websites, as well as personal experience and involvement with businesses, Pregnancy Resource Centers and Non-profit organizations have contributed to the thoughts, ideas and historical accounts set forth in **Change the Shame.**

Some of the major contributing sources include:

BOOKS—

Sounding Forth the Trumpet by Peter Marshal and David Manuel

The Civil War Almanac by John Bowman

13 Jars by Rob Fischer

Third Time Around by George Grant

The Cure by John Lynch

Why Pro-Life? by Randy Alcorn

Innocent Blood by John Ensor

Living in Color by Jenny McDermid

Hurt by Chap Clark

Answering the Call by John Ensor

Changed by Michaelene Fredenburg

You Lost Me by David Kinnaman

VIDEO—

YouTube
Schindler's List

WEBSITES—

YouTube.com

Wikipedia.org

USAWatchDog.com

NationalBlackProLifeUnion.com

3801Lancaster.com

ProLifeAction.org

Currently Perry Underwood
has written only one other book, **Webmertise**.

Webmertise is a book on
Electronic and Internet marketing.

More information about **Webmertise**
can be found on
Webmertise.com.